The Journey *of*
Forgiveness

How Forgiving Them Sets You Free

Tony Ingrassia

Unless otherwise indicated, all scripture quotations are taken from the Holy Bible, New International Version©. NIV ©. Copyright © 1973, 1978, 1984 by the International Bible Society.

ISBN # 978-0-9965731-1-5

For more information contact:

Tony Ingrassia at tony@powerofpurity.org

Cover and Interior Design by Janelle Evangelides

Preliminary book editing by Tracey Barski

Cartoon illustrations by Michelle Vrbka

The Journey of Forgiveness diagram by Kimberly Easton

Table of Contents

Introduction

I may not know you, but I know something very important about you. I know you've been deeply and profoundly hurt by another person, probably more than once in your lifetime, because it's virtually impossible to live in this very broken world without being hurt in this way. If I asked you to take a moment to reflect upon the historical landscape of your life, to identify a person that deeply hurt and betrayed you, could you identify that person? Who are they? Do you remember what happened? Do you remember what they said or what they did that hurt you so deeply? Did you try to forgive that person for what they did? Did you struggle with forgiving them? Did you "forgive" them, only to turn around and find feelings like resentment, bitterness, hatred, and even desires for revenge still alive and powerful within your own head and heart? Did you ever feel like you must be a really bad forgiver? If you can relate to any of these thoughts, you're like me in many ways because these are the very things I've struggled with on my journey of forgiveness.

In this book, I'm sharing the most difficult struggle with forgiveness I've ever experienced in my life. It's been a profoundly painful and difficult struggle, but one that's been very necessary, because ultimately, I realized I was being destroyed by my inability to forgive. As the old saying goes: *"Unforgiveness is like you drinking poison and hoping they die."* That's a really silly thing to do because, when you drink the poison, you're the one who dies, not them.

I realized I was being destroyed by my inability to forgive.

As my story unfolded, I struggled with the deepest betrayal, hurt, pain, and trauma I've ever experienced in my entire life, and I couldn't make the corresponding torment stop. I couldn't believe this person, whom I loved and trusted so much, did to me what they did. My soul was bleeding, and I basically cried my way through the first year as I grieved deeply. I was going to therapy in my attempt to process what had happened and, at one point, my therapist told me I was the most traumatized person she had ever worked with because of a broken relationship. The struggle went on and on, and I often felt as if I was suffocating from the difficulty and anguish of the situation.

As time passed, I kept turning to God and crying out to him for his mercy and his help. I developed a new spiritual discipline during this time where I was pouring my heart out to the Lord, and I was writing prayers, psalms, rants, and laments to him. I had written literally hundreds of these psalms to him. And it was only then, after struggling through the most difficult and painful period of my entire life, that God showed me, through an unusual series of events which I'll be sharing with you, the way for me to find true release, freedom, and peace of mind. But it wasn't at all what I expected God to show me because he showed me that I had to *forgive* this person. It was forgiveness that would lead to my freedom and unforgiveness that would leave me in the horrible place of bondage and torment in which I had been living for almost two years.

When I understood this, it became clear I had no other option because I sincerely knew I couldn't continue forward on the dark path I had been walking. It was destroying me because I was the one who had been drinking the poison. I was afraid that I would never be able to forgive them because I felt so much hurt and pain after what they had done to me. It felt like God was asking me to do something that was impossible, but I promised God I would try to forgive this person if he would show me how to do it. And that was the beginning of my journey of forgiveness.

As I began moving forward on the journey, God began to show me what he wanted me to do, one step at a time. It was as if he was saying, *"Tony, this is the next steppingstone on your journey of forgiveness. I want you to focus on this next step. I want you to think about this, and pray about this, and write about this, and process this, and struggle with this."* So I would work on that particular step, and then God would show me the next step, then the next step, then the next step, and so forth as he led me through the process.

In the end, I identified at least thirteen significant stepping-stones that were intrinsic to my journey of forgiveness, and those are represented in thirteen chapters in part two of this book. It should be noted that the way the steppingstones un-folded for me is not necessarily the way I'm presenting them within this book, and I've arranged them here in a sequence that seems to make them flow most naturally. I don't assume, by the way, that my journey of forgiveness is the same path that everyone else needs to follow. I'm simply sharing how God led me on *my* journey, and I pray that some of what I've been learning might be helpful or encouraging to you if you also have your own journey of forgiveness that you've been traveling or that you need to travel.

I'd like to establish, with absolute clarity, at least one other important point from the outset. As you'll learn, the context of the very hurtful situation that led to the writing of this book was what I consider the betrayal of the single most important relationship of my entire life. By writing about my need to forgive this person, I'm in no way proclaiming my own in-nocence. I'm not suggesting that I'm an innocent victim of everything that happened. This person profoundly hurt me and sinned against me in many ways, but I freely acknowledge that in the context of the relationship, I also hurt them and sinned against them in many ways. In fact, I'm 100% sure that throughout the course of the 40 plus years of my relationship with this person, that at various times I hurt them deeply, and

I was unkind to them, and selfish, and inconsiderate, and insensitive, and on and on it goes, and because of this they could, no doubt, write a book concerning their own journey of forgiveness toward me. But that's not the purpose of this book. The purpose of this book is for me to share the story of how I'm learning to forgive a person who hurt me more than I've ever been hurt in my entire life. It's been suggested that by writing this book my motive is to "trash" the person I'm writing about, but that isn't true at all, and in fact, if that were my motive, I could disclose the details of the entire story, and it would probably make them look much worse than anything I've actually written. My focus, therefore, will not be as much on the details of the story itself as much as the struggle that was raging in my own heart and life as a result. I'm not interested in attacking, blaming, shaming, or vilifying any other person, but I am interested in sharing my story in the hope it might be helpful and encouraging to others.

In the end, I felt I was supposed to write this book as a way for me to process what I've been learning and to embed the ideas and principles of forgiveness even deeper in my own heart and life. Because of this, I'm really writing to myself, but you're invited to eavesdrop on what Tony's writing to Tony, if you'd like to do so.

Unforgiveness is like you drinking poison and hoping they die.

I'm presenting this book in two main sections. Section One is entitled, *Tony's Story*, and I'm beginning with my story for a reason. I want to convey the profound pain that lived in my heart because of how deeply I was hurt by this person. Section Two is entitled, *The Journey of Forgiveness*, and in this section, I share the pathway of forgiveness that God revealed to me, one step at a time. I think it's important that you first understand the depth of my hurt and pain, so you understand exactly what I was trying to forgive as I began to walk on my journey of forgiveness.

I pray my story might be helpful and encouraging to you.

Part One

Tony's Story

One
My Deepest Hurt

Come to me, all you who are weary and
burdened, and I will give you rest.
Matthew 11:28

It was the most hurtful and devastating thing that ever happened to me. On July 6th, 2021, my wife left me after thirty-seven years of marriage. It was on a Tuesday, and we were at our regular counseling session with our therapist. We had been going to therapy for the previous year and a half to work on the challenges in our marriage that were exposed in large part by the very difficult circumstances we were facing in our relationships with our adult children.

As the session began, my wife, Sheri, took out a piece of paper and said she needed to read what she had written. After expressing several of her thoughts and struggles, the letter concluded by saying her car was already packed, and she was leaving immediately to go and stay with her mother. She didn't even wait until the end of our session. She just got up and walked out the door and out of my life. In retrospect, I don't think it was a coincidence that she left on that day because the next day, July 7th, was her sixtieth birthday. I think it was calculated, and I think she wanted a new and different life beginning with the first day of her sixth decade on planet earth. I had a surprise party planned for her special day with over sixty guests scheduled to attend. But that party never happened.

After thirty-seven years of marriage, my wife literally walked out of my life, and twenty-eight days later, she sent me a text to inform me she had hired an attorney and was filing for divorce. And that was it. After thirty-seven years of marriage, that's what I got. A text.

I was completely and utterly devastated in every way, and my heart was broken. My wife leaving me and filing for divorce has absolutely been the most difficult, painful, and traumatic thing I've ever experienced, and that's saying a lot because I've had a lot of terrible things happen in my life. For the next two years, as I waited for the divorce to be finalized, I prayed my wife might have a change of heart because I did not believe the divorce was the heart, mind, or will of God for our lives. I was in therapy for myself the entire time (and still am at the time of this writing) and, at one point, my therapist told me I was the most traumatized person she's ever seen because of a divorce.

I believe a person's soul can bleed on the inside when it gets hurt, just like a person's body can bleed on the outside, and my soul was definitely bleeding. I felt like I was on a roller coaster those first two years. As I grieved, I struggled deeply with feelings like loneliness, fear, anger, anxiety, depression, bitterness, self-hatred, and the even darker thoughts and feelings such as thoughts of self-harm and the desire for vengeance. When I'm upset, I can't eat because I don't have an appetite. When Sheri left me, I basically didn't eat for the first three weeks, and over the months to come I ended up losing a total of forty-five pounds. In the early weeks, I was also unable to sleep, and when I did, I would frequently have horrible nightmares.

My doctor gave me a prescription of Ambien in the attempt to help me rest. I'm sure I cried more tears during those two years than I had cried in my entire lifetime, and several of my good friends and family became very concerned about me. At one point, my brother told me I looked so bad that I looked like I had cancer.

I loved my wife with all my heart. I adored her. I was completely and radically devoted to her, to our marriage and to our wedding vows, and I never thought our marriage could come to an end. If God would have given me a choice, I would have been willing to lose anything in my life but Sheri. *"Take my legs, God, but don't take Sheri away from me. Take my eyesight, God, but don't take Sheri. Take all my money, God, and all my physical possessions. Take my farm away from me, and take my health, Lord, but don't take Sheri."*

We had been through so much during our thirty-seven-year marriage, but God had always been so faithful to us. The early years of our marriage were a complete disaster. We had been to hell and back, but we had done a lot of counseling over the years. God had done so much in both our lives and our marriage. This world is so crazy, and relationships can be so hard sometimes. They require so much work, but we had God, and we had each other, and I thought Sheri was the one person I could count on, no matter what. Even if the mountains fell into the sea, I knew Sheri would always be there for me. It was Sheri and me all the way, and I couldn't imagine my life without her. She gave me the most important promise of my life on September 17th, 1983, and I built my life upon her promise.

One time, years earlier, we had been sued by the person we sold a house to ten years before. It was a completely unfounded lawsuit, but this person was suing us for $400,000. The lawsuit took over two years and $60,000 to defend. When we finally went to trial, our attorney told us to expect the trial to last two days, but it lasted four full days. When the jury final-

She gave me the most important promise of my life on September 17th, 1983 and I built my life upon her promise.

ly went into deliberation, Sheri and I waited anxiously in the lobby of the courthouse. After a couple hours of waiting, our attorney finally appeared and notified us that the jury had arrived at their verdict, and it was time to go back into the courtroom. As we approached the majestic wooden doors leading back into the court, I hesitated because I wanted to say some words to my beautiful wife. I remember to this day what I said as I looked into her eyes: *"No matter what happens in there, we're going to be alright because we have the Lord and we have each other, and that's all that matters."* Not that it matters toward the purpose of this writing, but the verdict was twelve to zero in our favor.

When Sheri left me, I didn't know a person's heart could be so broken, and I didn't know a person could hurt so bad on the inside. I was wounded and confused. I felt betrayed. I felt overwhelmed. I felt disoriented and afraid. I felt discouraged and depressed and alone. I felt abandoned and rejected. I felt misunderstood and judged. I wondered who Tony was now because we had been Tony *and* Sheri for so long, I didn't know if I knew how to be Tony without Sheri by my side. If you could add up all the hurt and pain I was feeling in a big heap and throw all the other horrible thoughts and feelings I was struggling with onto the pile, I can't even imagine how big the mountain would be.

Waves crash upon the beach one after the other, and in much the same way, the waves of grief crashed upon my heart for the weeks and months and then years to come. Waves come then subside in a matter of time. But then another comes and another and another and another, and you wonder if it's ever going to end. If my biggest enemy conspired to harm both my heart and my life as deeply as possible, they could never design a more perfect plan to perpetrate upon me than what Sheri's choices and actions accomplished.

The five traditional stages of grief are denial, bargaining, anger, depression, and acceptance. And I guess if there's any good news here, it's the hope that we can eventually work our way to the acceptance of the difficult thing that's happened in our life. I don't necessarily think that means that we'll ever be alright with what's happened, but at least the unbearable darkness and pain begins to subside with time.

If you had a child die, your life would never be the same. You'd probably think of your child every day for the rest of your life, but you'd eventually work your way to acceptance because you wouldn't have any other choice. You'd have to accept the reality that your child is gone, and you'd have to find the grace of God that could help you to go on in your life with only the memory of your child.

One of the realities of grief is that these five stages are not linear in nature but are rather cyclical. As the waves of grief crash upon your heart, one after the other, you randomly cycle over and over again through the various stages in no particular order. Sometimes it makes you feel like you might be crazy because you're very angry one day, but then the anger subsides. You might feel deeply depressed for a week, then you find yourself denying the reality of what's happened. Then you feel depressed again, and then angry again. Round and round she goes, over and over again. I grieved in this way for well over the first year after Sheri left. Eventually, I very slowly began to flirt with the possibility of acceptance. I would have short periods of time where my heart felt a kind of reprieve as I tried to reconcile myself with the reality of what had happened. I began to experience brief periods of relief and even peace.

Throughout this time, I accidently developed a new spiritual discipline that became very helpful and encouraging to me. I began to write out my own prayers and psalms to the Lord. When I was upset, I would write to the Lord and tell him I was upset. When I was confused or depressed, I would write to the Lord to tell him what I was struggling with. When I felt terrible, or I felt like giving up, or when I felt the ugliness of my

own resentment or bitterness, I would write to the Lord and tell him what I was feeling and what I was struggling with. If I felt angry at Sheri, which was quite often, I would write to the Lord, and if I felt angry at myself, I would write to the Lord, and if I felt angry at God, I would write to him and tell him.

I was learning to bring my pain and my wounded heart to the Lord. I was learning to turn to God, to run to God, and to confide in God. As I developed this new spiritual discipline, it often became the only way I knew to escape the feelings of torment I was experiencing, to find a sense of relief and reprieve. At the time of this writing, I've now written over six hundred of these psalms, and I can't imagine where I might be today if I had not learned to bring my pain to God in this way. I'll be sharing a few of those psalms with you throughout the remainder of this book.

I was learning to turn to God, to run to God, and to confide in God.

Two
The Rendezvous Café

*It's not an enemy who taunts me - I could bear that.
It's not my foes who so arrogantly insult me - I could
have hidden from them. Instead, it is you - my equal,
my companion and close friend.*
Psalm 55:12-13

As I approached the two-year anniversary of my wife leaving and filing for divorce, I was still grieving, but I felt as if I was cycling in and out of acceptance on a more regular basis. I was still praying my wife might have a change of heart, but I had not seen even one half of one inch of movement from her in any way. I had written to her and appealed to her over and over again, especially during the first year after she left me. (To hear more about the appeals I made to my wife, listen to Episode 371 of The Power of Purity Podcast, entitled Tony's Divorce Appeal.) But she never responded in any way except with resistance, and mostly with complete silence. I told her how much I loved her and how committed and devoted I was to her and to our marriage, but she didn't even seem to care. I asked her to please go to counseling with me, but she refused. I asked her to please present to me a list of whatever she would need from me in order to join me in the fight for our marriage, but she refused to do so. I found a counseling service that offers a special intensive for marriages in crisis toward the hope of averting divorce, but she refused to attend the intensive with me. It appeared there was no hope for our marriage whatsoever, and it seemed obvious that my wife was determined to have her divorce.

I love the wisdom of the Serenity Prayer when it says we should ask God to help us change the things we can change, to accept the things we cannot change, and the wisdom to know the difference. In view of this, I needed to acknowledge and accept the reality that I was completely powerless to change my wife in any way.

I couldn't change what she was thinking and believing. I couldn't change what she wanted and what she was choosing, and in this way, I was completely powerless to change the reality of the situation. The only person I had any control over whatsoever was myself, and I was trying very hard to accept the reality that my wife was truly gone.

After almost two years, I was very slowly making progress in my attempt to accept the situation, to reconcile myself with the reality of my new life without my wife, and it seemed as if I was finally getting a little traction and making a little forward progress toward acceptance. That is until a close friend of mine, Charlotte, invited me to have lunch with her one day. Little did I know how dramatically that lunch would bring the dark pain that still lived in my heart to a crescendo.

Charlotte is a ministry associate of mine and had been a friend to both Sheri and me for many years. As part of The Power of Purity ministry I'm involved in, I present a three-day weekend intensive for men on the topic of sexual purity.

At this conference, I share with men information, tools, and strategies that will empower them to experience their sexual gift in a healthier way as they learn to bring their sexual gift under the authority of Christ. (For more information about The Power of Purity visit www.powerofpurity.org) Charlotte often helps me on these intensive weekends when I have her present a session for the men on the topic of "betrayal trauma." This session helps the men to understand the hurt and pain their wife has experienced as a result of sexual betrayal and how to regain both their wife's heart and trust again. While I could present this session myself, I believe there's great value in the men hearing and experiencing the session through what I call the "voice of Eve," and Charlotte always does a wonderful job.

We had just finished a very powerful session at an intensive on a Sunday afternoon, and as I helped Charlotte carry her things to her car, she asked me if we could have lunch "sooner than later." She said she needed to talk to me about something important, and I could tell there was a sense of urgency in her voice. I wondered what might be wrong, and we scheduled ourselves to have lunch the very next day, which was a Monday.

When we met for lunch, we chitchatted for a bit. Finally, Charlotte told me that she had some bad news that she didn't want to tell me but felt that she needed to share. I couldn't image what she needed to say, and she had my complete attention.

Charlotte told me that she had been out at a local restaurant with some friends on the previous Saturday evening, The Rendezvous Café, and while they were there, they saw my wife Sheri there with another man. She was apparently on a date with this man. When Charlotte saw this, she immediately felt disturbed, and she wasn't quite sure exactly how to respond in the situation.

As I mentioned previously, Charlotte had been good friends with both Sheri and me for several years, and when Sheri first left me, Charlotte reached out to Sheri, and they met together at least one time. Charlotte's heart was to advocate to Sheri on behalf of our marriage, and after that initial meeting, Sheri refused to meet with Charlotte again.

I needed to acknowledge and accept the reality that I was completely powerless to change my wife in any way.

I suspect that was for at least two different reasons. One is that Sheri knew that Charlotte stood in opposition to her chosen path toward divorce, and two, because of my professional relationship and connection with Charlotte, Sheri probably assumed that Charlotte was defending an alliance and loyalty to "Team Tony".

To make the situation at the restaurant even more awkward, Charlotte was coincidently seated at the table right next to Sheri, and they were so close to each other they could almost literally touch one another. Because of this, Charlotte quickly decided within herself that the best way to play the situation was head on, so she finally turned around to both acknowledge and greet Sheri.

"Oh, my goodness! Sheri! How are you? It's so good to see you. How have you been?" Charlotte could tell Sheri seemed uncomfortable at her greeting, and as they chitchatted for several moments, it seemed quite awkward for everyone involved. At one point during the brief conversation Sheri introduced the gentleman friend she was having dinner with. They exchanged just a few more pleasantries and the conversation concluded when Charlotte touched Sheri with both of her hands, one on Sheri's left forearm and one on her left shoulder, and said, *"Sheri, it was so good to see you, and I'd really like to get together and talk if you would ever like to do so."* With that, Charlotte turned around and sat back down with her party. There are at least three other noteworthy things about this encounter that should be mentioned.

First, as the evening unfolded, at one point, Sheri and this man both stood up. They raised their glasses of wine to one another in an apparent toast, and they then leaned over the table and kissed one another.

Second, there were about ten people at the table that Charlotte was having dinner with. One of these women, completely oblivious to the situation with Sheri, was taking various pictures throughout the evening, and later that night posted her pictures on Facebook. And again, coincidently, there were at least a couple different pictures that showed Charlotte with both Sheri and this man in the immediate background. So not only did I get to hear this story from Charlotte, but I actually got to see the pictures of Sheri and this man together along with their nice glasses of wine.

And third, both coincidently and ironically, the pictures revealed that above the table where Sheri and this man were sitting was a big sign with only one word that was very conspicuous: *"FAMILY"*. As Charlotte shared the story of meeting Sheri at The Rendezvous Café, I sat in stunned silence. Charlotte told me she hadn't wanted to tell me the story because she knew it would hurt me. But as my friend, she felt she had to disclose to me what had happened, as well as the truth about the kiss and the pictures that revealed Sheri and this man together. I had already been living for the past two years with the metaphorical knife that had been plunged deep within my heart by what my wife had done, but as I listened to Charlotte's story and saw the corresponding pictures, I could feel the knife twisting even deeper in my heart than ever before.

You'd think this information would not have been so powerfully hurtful to me because my wife had already been gone for almost two years, but somehow, the knowledge that she was now with another man, and especially the knowledge of the kiss she shared with that man, only served to radically intensify my pain and grief.

I love the wisdom of the Serenity Prayer when it says we should ask God to help us change the things we can change, to accept the things we cannot change, and the wisdom to know the difference.

Chapter #2

Three

The Green Beast

Deep calls to deep in the roar of your waterfalls;
all your waves and breakers have swept over me.
Psalm 42:7

Even though we had been separated for almost two years, Sheri was still my wife, and the knowledge that she was in some kind of a relationship with another man was almost unbearable to me. When Charlotte shared the story with me, it set in motion a sequence of events that made the days to follow among the most difficult and darkest of my entire life. It's as if the next metaphorical wave of grief crashed on the beach of Tony's heart, only this wave seemed bigger and more powerful than almost all that had come before.

Coincidentally, I spent an entire day with my oldest son the following week, and during that time, we talked a little bit about the situation. I asked my son if he knew about this man. My son responded by saying that he was trying to stay out of the situation, but that he was *"aware of this person"* his mother was involved with. Based upon my son's comments, I drew some conclusions, although I fully recognize that those conclusions were based upon both speculation and assumption. What I concluded in my own head and heart, was that Sheri's relationship with this man had been going on for some period of time, and that it was apparently a pretty serious relationship.

I based these assumptions upon at least a couple different observations that I was suspicious of. I figured that if The Rendezvous Café was Sheri's first date with this man, or among their first couple dates, she probably would not be celebrating a "toast" and a kiss with him in public, and she probably wouldn't go above and beyond the call of duty to inform our sons that she was dating this particular man. The fact that my son knew about this man made me suspicious that maybe he had been around for a while. Why else would my son know about him? It made me wonder if my son had ever met him. Had Sheri brought him over to my son's house to visit with my son and his family? Had they ever been to dinner together? Had Sheri brought him to a family get together where I wasn't invited? If my oldest son was *"aware of this person,"* were my other sons also *"aware of this person?"* It was the conglomeration of all these thoughts and speculations that began to relentlessly torment both my heart and my thoughts in the days that followed.

What I'm about to share next might reveal what a terrible and twisted person I am, but I'm just honestly sharing as transparently as I can the reality of the thoughts and feelings I was struggling with at the time. I knew my wife had shared the intimacy of a kiss with another man, and that reality led my mind to cascade, like a series of never-ending dominos through an escalating sequence of thoughts and questions. If my wife was willing to share the intimacy of a kiss with this man in public, what intimacies was she willing to share with him in private? Was she allowing him to hold her and to caress her hair? How deep were her feelings for him, and had she ever spoken the words *"I love you"* to him? I wondered if she ever invited him to spend time with her in the apartment she had set up in her mother's basement, and I wondered what might be happening in the apartment if that was the case. In respect of her mother, if she never invited him to visit her in the basement apartment, had she ever gone to his house to be alone with him? They had met at The Rendezvous Café, and I wondered if they had ever had any other private and clandestine "rendezvous". Were they, in fact, sharing the ultimate intimacies with one another? The thoughts of Sheri sharing such intimacy with another man was very upsetting to me, especially since I, myself, had remained true to the Holy Vow I had made to both Sheri and the Lord some twenty-four years earlier when I promised I would not express or experience my sexual gift apart from her as my wife. Since she had left me two years earlier, although I struggled at times, I continued to honor my Holy Vow to her, and I had not looked at pornography or allowed myself to have an orgasm even one single time for the past two years. It was the single longest sexual fast of my entire life.

In the interest of full disclosure, I have to admit that by this time, I had also been on a couple dates with women, although I would not really call them official "dates," and in view of that, I can't sit in judgment of my wife having a social visit with another man. We had, after all, been separated for almost two full years at this point.

Along the way, I had been encouraged by several of the trusted confidants and advisors in my life, including my counselor, to go ahead and allow myself to meet a couple women for conversation. I wondered if I should do that since I was still legally married to Sheri, but I was encouraged to consider doing so.

"Your wife is gone Tony. She's made her decision, and the divorce is nothing more than a legal technicality at this point. You're not looking to get married, and you're not even looking for a serious relationship, so what's it going to hurt to meet a couple women for coffee, and to have some conversation?"

So, in view of this advice, I placed a bio on a Christian dating site, and I did meet with a couple different nice ladies. But as this unfolded over a short period of time, I felt completely uncomfortable, and I simply couldn't continue to do it. So I canceled my bio, I continued to pray that my wife might have a change of heart, and I certainly didn't touch or kiss any woman whatsoever.

After learning about Sheri and this man at the lunch with Charlotte, the cascade of disturbing and upsetting thoughts and images flooded though my mind for the days that followed. Like watching a movie on the big screen in the theater of my mind, pornographic scenes of my wife doing everything imaginable with another man played endlessly on and on. Of course, I didn't know if any such things were happening, but I couldn't stop my mind from the imaginations.

"I wonder if they've ever done this? I wonder if they've ever done that? I wonder if she's ever done such and such to him? I wonder if she's ever let him do such and such to her? I wonder if they've ever done such and such, which her and I used to do?"

I tried to make the thoughts and images stop. I tried to push them aside. I tried to ignore them. I prayed and asked God to take them away from me. But it seemed like the harder I tried to escape them, the stronger and more vivid the thoughts and images became. At times I felt absolutely tormented, and I wondered if I might literally be going crazy.

In the way of metaphor, I felt like I was a man who had fallen off a ship, overboard into a dark and tumultuous sea. In the effort to survive I had been treading water for a long time (for about two years) as I fought desperately to keep my face above the violent waters. I was completely exhausted, and I didn't know how much longer I could continue to fight for my own survival. And then, of all things, this green and scaly monster swims up to me with the malevolent intention to drown me. This beast is huge. He's way bigger than me, and way stronger. He has beady black eyes and pointed ears and claws and fangs, and he's slobbering at the mouth. He swims up to me while

I'm desperately struggling to keep my face above the water and, much to my horror, he climbs on top of me and begins to violently push and dunk me under the water. I'm terrified. I don't know what to do. I'm thrashing. This is impossible. I'm struggling and fighting with all my might to get back to the surface for just one more gasp of air, but I know I can't win this battle. Panic is gripping me. I'm suffocating, and it feels like I'm hopelessly doomed, and I have absolutely no chance of survival. There's a sense of panic and desperation gripping me. What am I going to do, and where do I go from here?

chapter 3

Four
Break the Chains and Cut the Nets

Then they cried to the Lord in their trouble, and he saved
them from their distress. He brought them out of darkness,
the utter darkness, and broke away their chains.
Psalm 107:13-14

It was on a Monday when I had lunch with Charlotte, and she told me about The Rendezvous Café. I felt quite upset and struggled for two days in the attempt to get my equilibrium. Two days later, on Wednesday, Charlotte called to check in with me and to see how I was doing. We had a long talk, and I shared my struggle with her, telling her about the metaphorical green beast that climbed on top of me and was trying to drown me. During that conversation, Charlotte said two different things that became significant to me. One was about "chains" and the other was about "nets."

I have this odd gifting that enables me to see pictures and metaphors, and it happens all the time. I'm not saying I'm prophetic, but I just continuously get pictures and metaphors that enable me to see, understand, and to communicate something deeper about what's being said, or to describe various thoughts and feelings or ideas and concepts. An example of one such metaphor was the green beast himself. I had been feeling terrible for the previous two days, and I was struggling deeply with the thoughts and images that I couldn't turn off. It was then that I saw the picture of myself as the man who had fallen into the deep and turbulent water that was way over my head, and the powerful green beast that had scales and claws and fangs which climbed on top of me and was trying to drown me. So when Charlotte mentioned both "chains" and "nets," I could immediately see dramatic images of both ideas.

It had been almost two years since Sheri had left me, and Charlotte commented that it was as if there were these invisible chains enslaving me to Sheri that had to be broken, so I could escape. She said the chains were so strong that I could never break them by myself, and that I needed someone more powerful and much stronger than me to break the chains on my behalf. In addition, she said it was as if I was entangled in a big net, like a big fishing net, and the more I struggled to escape the net, the more entangled and trapped I had become. Charlotte said that when you're entangled in a net, you can't free yourself. You need someone else from the outside to cut the nets so you can escape, and of course, the only person who could cut the nets to set me free was the Lord himself. These images of the chains and nets were very powerful to me and would become very significant as I began to spontaneously and continuously pray a prayer for the next several days. It seemed to emerge from deep within me, like a kind of rhythmic spiritual breathing.

"Dear God, please break the chains and cut the nets that I'm entangled in. Please help me, Lord. These chains and nets are stronger than me, Lord. I can't get free. Please help me, oh God. Please do for me what I can't do for myself. Please break these chains and cut these nets. I need you, oh God."

After my conversation with Charlotte on that Wednesday, I wrote a psalm to the Lord entitled "Break the Chains and Cut the Nets", but I'm not sharing that psalm here.

Chapter #4

A couple more days passed, and it was now Friday. It had been five days since I learned of The Rendezvous Café, and two days since my conversation with Charlotte on Wednesday. I had been continuously praying that God would "break the chains and cut the nets," but much to my dismay, my struggle was only deepening.

It seemed as if an intense battle was raging all around me and the fury of hell was unleashed against me. Instead of getting better, the weight I was carrying was only getting heavier, and the darkness around me was only getting darker. The horrible thoughts and images were still pummeling me, and the green beast on top of me seemed to be getting stronger as I was getting weaker. I felt like a total zombie by the time Friday arrived. I was numb. I felt so hurt. I was confused. I was very upset. I was depressed. I was struggling with very dark thoughts of anger, bitterness, hatred, and thoughts and feelings of self-harm and vengeance. The shadow self that lives in me occasionally fantasized about perpetrating harm upon the one who had hurt me so deeply with the expectation that if I could hurt her bad enough that maybe I'd no longer hurt so bad. Of course, the natural proclivity of the shadow self is very misguided, cannot be trusted, and is completely inconsistent with the way of God's Kingdom. But when you're in the heat of the battle, you can't always see the situation you're in with either clarity or objectivity. Maybe that's because the shadow self casts long and dark shadows that cause everything around you to become blurred and confused.

It's very hard to put words to what that Friday was like for me, the day I now affectionately refer to as "Dark Friday." Not so much because I couldn't describe it if I wanted to, but more from the fear that if I did honestly describe it, people might be completely horrified by the darkness that can live in Tony's heart and mind. Suffice to say that this day was a kind of crescendo to all the horrible days leading up to it and certainly among the hardest and most terrible days of my life.

When you're in the heat of the battle, you can't always see the situation you're in with either clarity or objectivity.

In John 10:10 Jesus said, "the thief comes to steal, kill, and destroy", and I believe evil was literally trying to close the deal on my life that day. When I finally got home late that evening, after a long and tiring day, I wonder in retrospect if I was having either a panic attack or a mental breakdown. I know I looked at my hands, and they were physically and uncontrollably shaking, and it took everything I had to try to talk myself off the ledge. It felt like I was drowning. The green beast was on top of me and he was suffocating me, and I was fighting to get my face above the water in my desperate attempt to get one last gasp of life-giving air.

I wrote a psalm to the Lord that evening entitled "Renunciation," and I'm sharing a redacted version of that psalm here.

Psalm 499 – Renunciation

Dear God,

Today is a very hard day, Lord.

I'm asking you to break the Sheri chains off of me, God.

Please cut me free from the Sheri nets.

I was doing slightly better the past two days, but today it crashed over me like a tidal wave.

This horrible thing trying to climb over me and smother me.

I'm tormented by the thought of my wife on her date with another man, enjoying their wine and kisses.

The picture is burned in my mind, and it keeps coming back to me.

My wife kissing another man, while I'm honoring her since the day she left me with my vow of purity to her.

It really hurts, Lord.

I can't do this, oh God.

It will crush me.

It will destroy me.

I have to get this off of me, God.

I have to get free of it.

But I can't, Lord.

It's too big for me.

It's way more powerful than me.

How can I stand in front of a tidal wave and not have it knock me over and not get soaking wet?

It makes me think the dark thoughts, Lord.

Please help me, God.

I need you to do for me what I cannot do for myself.

Please break the chains, and please cut me out of the nets, Lord.

I'd like to renounce her, Lord, but I'm afraid to do that.

I'm afraid because I made a promise to her and to you.

How can I renounce my own wife and my precious wedding vows?

But I'm tempted to renounce her, Lord.

To renounce her as my wife.

To renounce our wedding vows.

To renounce our marriage.

To renounce what she's done to me.

I don't know how to stop being hurt by it, Lord.

I don't know how to stop caring about it.

I don't know how to get free of it.

It's like invisible chains and invisible nets.

And I'm chained to her, and I'm trapped by her.

And I need to get free, oh God.

Please help me, Lord.

So I do not renounce her, Lord, because I can't, and I do not renounce our wedding vows, because I can't, but I do renounce the chains and the nets that I'm trapped in.

Please renounce the chains and the nets oh God.

Please, oh please, oh God.

It's like I'm being cut in half, and I don't know how to be cut in half.

I'm asking you, Lord, and crying out to you to please shatter and crush these chains, and please cut these nets, oh God.

The thoughts and images come to me, and they drag me under the surface like heavy balls and chains, where I can't breathe.

It's suffocating, Lord.

It drives me crazy to think these things.

I can't go on and on with these thoughts and images.

It's too much, Lord.

It hurts too much.

It's too tormenting.

Is there something seriously wrong with me, Lord?

Please help me to let her go, Lord.

She left me.

She left our marriage.

She's broken our wedding vows, and I can't see at least two very important things, Lord.

I can't see that it's your will for us to get divorced.

You, the God who makes very clear what you say about divorce in your Holy Word, and you, the God who says he hates divorce because it's the violent ripping apart of the one flesh of marriage. (Malachi 2:16)

And I can't see that she has biblical grounds for her divorce, Lord.

She won't even talk to me about why she's done what she's done.

And the biggest complaint she has that I can identify is that I'm not a good "listener."

And even if that's true, Lord, you don't get divorced for that.

You work on that, and I'm willing to work on that, and we were in counseling for the past year and a half working on our relationship and marriage, and she even left me in a counseling session.

So it's not like I was unwilling to hear her, Lord, and to work on whatever she needed.

But she left me, Lord, after thirty-seven years of marriage, and she completely broke my heart.

She doesn't want me, Lord.

So I don't want to want her anymore.

It's too hard.

Please renounce the chains and the nets.

Please help me, Lord.

Please protect me with the blood of Christ.

In Jesus' Name I pray.

Amen.

Lord, I need you to do for me what I cannot do for myself.

Five
You're Going to Have to Forgive

But small is the gate and narrow the road that
leads to life, and only a few find it.
Matthew 7:14

The day after "Dark Friday," I was both mentally and emotionally exhausted. I knew I could not continue forward much longer on the trajectory I was presently on because if I did, I was either going to go crazy or die. How long, after all, can a person continue struggling in tumultuous dark waters while there's a powerful green beast on top of them trying to drown them? I, therefore, began crying out to the Lord in what might have been the deepest and most desperate cries and prayers of my life.

"Please help me, oh God. I feel like I'm drowning, Lord. I feel like I'm suffocating. I don't know where to go from here, Lord. What am I going to do? Please break the chains, Lord, and please cut the nets I'm entangled in. This is too big for me, Lord. I don't know how to set myself free. I don't know how to stop the thoughts and images on the inside of me. I need you to help me, Lord. I need you to rescue me. Please show me the way, Lord. How do I get out of these chains and nets?"

I was seeking God and begging God for help, and I knew I had no other option because where else was I going to go, and what else was I going to do? If I had the ability to set myself free from this darkness and torment, I would have already done it many months before, but I didn't know how to rescue myself, and I was desperately crying out to God to show me the way forward.

Unfortunately, this deep struggle went on for the next five tortuous days, and I wondered if there would ever be an end. Saturday, Sunday, Monday, Tuesday, and then Wednesday. But then, on Wednesday morning, it was as if the Lord finally began to crack open the door of heaven to begin showing me the answer to the prayer I had been so earnestly pleading to him, *but in a very unexpected way.*

I had a conversation with a dear friend of mine named CJ. CJ is a prayer warrioress in God's Kingdom, and she's prayed faithfully for both me and my ministry for many years. In addition, she had stood by my side over the past two years since my wife left by checking on me, supporting me, encouraging me, talking to me, listening to me, and by just being there for me in general. On this particular morning, CJ and I were talking on the phone, and the conversation suddenly became quite poignant when she said something that was unexpected and probably the very last thing I ever wanted to hear her say. In fact, the moment was so significant, I can remember exactly where I was. I was sitting in my car at the time, and although I didn't realize it in the moment, in retrospect, what CJ said became like the first domino in a chain of redemptive and healing dominos that were about to begin cascading through my heart and life.

"Tony, you're going to have to forgive Sheri."

When CJ said those words, I had a kneejerk and visceral reaction, and the words quite spontaneously leapt out of my mouth: *"There's absolutely no way in the world I can forgive Sheri because there's too much hurt and there's too much pain."*

And although those were the first words out of my mouth, it's as if those words were energized by a thousand other words and emotions that were all buried deep within my heart, in the same way there's the giant ninety-five percent of an iceberg that's lurking under the five percent of what you can see above the water.

"How in the world could I ever forgive Sheri after what she's done to me? How could I forgive her after she abandoned me and betrayed both me and our wedding vows? How could I forgive her when she's caused the deepest hurt and the deepest pain and deepest suffering and the greatest trauma of my entire life? How could I possibly forgive her when she's caused the past two years to be the darkest and most difficult time of my life? How could I ever forgive Sheri when she's broken the most important promise anyone has ever made to me? How could I possibly forgive her when she's hurt me more than any other person has ever hurt me, and she's caused my soul to bleed and bleed and bleed and bleed?"

I had been thinking something and feeling something very powerfully for quite some time, and I had shared it with several of my closest friends, and this thought and these feelings were very deep and real to me. I sincerely and passionately felt that I never wanted to see Sheri's face ever again in my entire lifetime. Why would I want to? Whenever a picture of her would somehow appear on my iPhone or on my Facebook page, it was like being stabbed in the heart, and I would immediately avert my eyes because I could barely stand to see her image. Her choices and her actions had cost me more and taken more away from my life than anything any other person had ever done to me. Because of Sheri, my entire life had been ripped in half. Everything I had worked so hard for so many years to provide for us was suddenly ripped in half and taken from me.

I was being forced to leave the home we had lived in for over twenty years, the home I loved, and I had to move into a house I didn't want to live in. If I wanted to keep the hunting property I loved so much, I was being forced to buy it back from my wife at the highest price it had ever been valued since I had bought it over twenty-five years before. If an enemy maliciously wanted to perpetrate harm and destruction upon my life, they could never do more to me than what Sheri had done to me, so why in the world would I ever want to be in the same room with that person or ever see their face again? I had thought to myself on more than one occasion, *"If my grandchildren ever get married, I'll never go to their weddings if Sheri is going to be there."*

I felt I could never see her again or ever look at her face again because, if I did, the knife that lived in my heart would be twisted so deep that I might literally die. I'm not proud of myself at all for feeling or saying any of these things, but it was very alive and powerful to me, and it's what I was feeling and struggling with at the time. You, therefore, might begin to comprehend why CJ's suggestion that I was going to have to forgive Sheri felt both repugnant and almost offensive to me in the moment. I thought to myself, *"She's done all this to me, but I have to forgive her? She's ripped my soul out, but I have to forgive her? She's caused me all this hurt and pain and torment, but I have to forgive her?"*

I had been a believer in Christ for almost fifty years, and I believed in the concept of forgiveness in my head. I was a graduate from both bible college and seminary, and I believed in forgiveness in my theology, and no doubt I could present a really good bible study on forgiveness or preach a really good sermon on forgiveness. But what makes for really good preaching sometimes makes for really hard living.

It felt like the hurt and pain and darkness that lived in me because of what Sheri had done to me was like a raging forest fire burning out of control, and the "forgiveness" I might be able to muster in myself was the equivalent to a teaspoon of water, if that. How in the world do you put out a raging forest fire with a teaspoon of water? I believed in forgiveness in my

PAIN   HURT   BETRAYAL   SUFFERING   TORMENT

FORGIVENESS

Chapter #5.

head and in my theology, but in the shadow of the deepest hurt and the greatest pain of my life, I had absolutely no idea how to make forgiveness work in my real-life situation. It simply seemed like it was impossible for me to do, and if that made me a terrible person and a terrible Christian, then I'm both a terrible person and a terrible Christian.

CJ and I talked about forgiveness for a short period of time, and I insisted the entire conversation that there was no way I could ever forgive Sheri. No way. The conversation then ended when CJ asked me if I would just think about it, and I promised her I would.

As evidence of the deep struggle I was feeling in my heart to ever forgive my wife, I wrote the following psalm, but please note that I wrote this psalm over a year before I ever had the conversation with CJ that I've shared in this chapter.

In the shadow of the deepest hurt and the greatest pain of my life, I had absolutely no idea how to make forgiveness work in my real-life situation.

Psalm 304 – I Don't Want to Forgive My Wife

Dear God,

I'm struggling tonight with feelings of anger and resentment toward my wife, whose name I do not want to write.

I'm feeling in my heart, Lord, and I have been feeling this for some time now, that I never ever want to see her again.

What she has done to me is much worse than what an arch enemy could ever do to hurt and harm my life.

If an arch enemy conspired to perpetrate maximum harm upon me, I don't think they could do more than what she's done to me.

I therefore feel that I cannot be around her, Lord.

I do not want to see her.

I do not want to be near her.

I'm struggling so deeply in my heart.

I feel like, if there's some kind of get together, like a birthday party for one of our grandchildren, that I couldn't go if I know she's going to be there.

I feel like, if the day comes that one of the girls is getting married, that I couldn't go if I know she's going to be there.

I feel like if she happened to die unexpectedly, that I couldn't go to her funeral, even though she was my wife for thirty-nine years.

And sometimes I've struggled with other thoughts, Lord, that I'm not even going to write on this page, but you know what they are.

And I know that as a Christian I'm supposed to forgive her.

While he was on the cross, Jesus said, *"Forgive them for they know not what they do."*

And I know that I'm supposed to forgive because I, myself, have been forgiven so much.

But forgiving her is inconceivable to me, Lord.

I'm sorry, Lord.

I'm sorry if you're disappointed in me.

I'm sorry that I'm such a lousy Christian.

I'm sorry that I'm so weak and so incapable of doing the very things that you say I should do.

I don't know if I can't forgive, or if I don't want to forgive.

And maybe it's both.

And right now, Lord, I don't think I even want to want to forgive her.

What she's done to me is so terrible, Lord.

It's just so terrible.

And it isn't even finished yet because it just goes on and on.

She walked out the door and never looked back.

She filed for divorce.

She ripped my soul out.

She's caused an incomprehensible amount of pain in my heart and life.

She's cutting me in half financially after I've worked so hard for us.

She's taking the house I love away from me.

She's forcing me to move someplace I don't want to move, to live someplace I don't want to live.

She's caused me to be forced into the single longest sexual fast of my life.

She's made me into a monster to herself, and to those around her, in order to justify to her own conscience what she's done to me.

But I'm not a monster, Lord.

I'm an imperfect man with faults and defects of character, but I'm a good man with a good heart, and I love you, Lord, and I serve you, and I help people, and I don't deserve what she's done to me.

She violated and betrayed the most important promise that anyone has ever made to me in my entire life.

I don't want to use the word "hate," Lord, because I'm trying not to hate her in my heart.

I pray that you will help me, Lord.

Do you understand what I'm struggling with?

Am I a horrible person, Lord, because I don't want to forgive my wife?

Am I a horrible person, Lord, because I don't want to forgive my wife?

Six

The Journey of Forgiveness

In all your ways acknowledge him, and
he will direct your paths.
Proverbs 3:6

I had talked to CJ on a Wednesday morning, and late that same evening, I was going through the credenza behind my desk in my home office, cleaning things out. Because of the impending divorce and the reality that I would soon be forced out of our home, I had slowly begun to go through all my things, to clean them out, throw things away, to organize and to pack things in preparation for the upcoming move.

I've always believed that moving is among the worst things a person must do in their life, and it was especially burdensome to me given the difficult and hurtful circumstances that were forcing me to move. The house I was moving into was substantially smaller than the house we had lived in for the past twenty years, and because of this I was absolutely determined to downsize and to get rid of as much stuff as I possibly could. As I went through the credenza, there were many things that had been in there for many years. The drawers were full of a variety of things, including old notebooks and journals, books, papers, and copies of old sermons and bible studies, pictures, files, old bank statements, DVDs, and even old cassette tapes, which evidenced how long many of those things had apparently been sitting in those drawers.

As I was going through the stack of papers I found in one of the drawers, my eyes fell upon a particular document, and the title on the top seemed to leap off the page and grab my attention: *Releasing Those Who Have Hurt Us.* It was a six-page document that was a copy of chapter six from a book written by Ed Smith entitled, *Theophostic Prayer Ministry.* The six pages were stapled together with three staples across the top edge of the paper. It's hard for me to describe exactly what happened in that moment, and all I can say is that I believe with all my heart that God anointed my eyes to see those six words. When I saw them, it's as if the Holy Spirit shot an arrow from his divine bow directly at my heart – *Releasing Those Who Have Hurt Us.* I immediately sensed and somehow knew that this paper coming into my hands at this very moment was not a coincidence. In view of the profoundly difficult situation I had been struggling with for the past two years, and in view of the intense crescendo of thoughts and emotions I had been struggling with for the past week since learning of The Rendezvous Café, and especially in light of the conversation I had with CJ that very morning, I knew the paper I was looking at in my hands at that moment was not an accident. It was, in fact, evidence of the very fingerprints of God on my life. What are the chances, after all, that I would have the conversation I had with CJ that very morning concerning forgiveness, and that I would then discover this paper that same evening after it had, no doubt, been sitting in my credenza for God only knows how many years?

In fact, it was weeks later that CJ disclosed to me that she had been impressed to talk to me about forgiveness for at least three weeks before she finally talked to me. It took her three weeks because she was nervous about how I would react to the topic, and she was afraid I might actually get mad at her for suggesting that I needed to forgive Sheri. Because of this reluctance, she waited and she prayed, and she waited and she prayed, and she waited and she prayed. Then coincidently, the day CJ finally found the courage to talk to me about forgiveness just happened to be the very same day that I would find the chapter of Ed Smith's book in the credenza.

So when both of those things happened on the same day, it got my attention. I sensed in my heart, and I knew that I knew that I knew that God had brought this paper to me and that he wanted me to read it. I, therefore, finished up what I was doing, then went to sit in the spot where I spend time with the Lord, and where I write most of my psalms, and I slowly read the chapter.

The topic focused on a review of the parable of the unforgiving servant that Jesus taught in Matthew 18:21-35. In the chapter, Smith shares seven different observations from the parable. Jesus presents the parable in response to Peter's question, *"How many times should I forgive my brother when he sins against me? Up to seven times?"* Jesus responds by telling Peter, *"I tell you, not seven times, but seventy times seven,"* and then goes on to teach the parable. The parable itself is the story of a servant who was forgiven a debt of ten thousand bags of gold that he could never repay his master, but this servant then turns around and refuses to forgive a fellow servant who owes him a debt of only one hundred pieces of silver. It's a beautiful and amazing parable, and it provides significant insights to both the heart and the Kingdom of God.

As I read it, there was such a powerful confirmation happening in my heart, and I knew that God was directly answering the prayers I had so desperately been asking of Him. I felt that God was very clearly saying to me, *"This is the way forward, Tony. This is the answer to your prayers. This is the way out of your darkness and torment. This is how to get the green monster off you. This is how I'm going to break the chains and cut the nets. You need to forgive Sheri, and when you forgive Sheri, you're the one who will be set free."*

This is how I'm going to break the chains and cut the nets. You need to forgive Sheri, and when you forgive Sheri, you're the one who will be set free.

After reading the paper God had placed in my hands, I then-wrote a psalm to the Lord, and the following is a redacted version of that psalm

Psalm 505 – Freedom Comes Through Forgiveness

Dear God,

I think you might be showing me something very significant, Lord.

Maybe this is the answer to what I've been asking you for, to break the chains that are holding me enslaved to my soon-to-be ex-wife, and the nets I've been entangled in.

And wouldn't you know that in a mystery, it reveals something of your inside out, upside down, backwards, and paradoxical Kingdom.

It concerns forgiveness, Lord, and the implication that I need to forgive Sheri, and that forgiveness is the thing that will set me free from the chains and nets.

Today I spoke with CJ on the phone, and she challenged me pretty strongly on some things, and one of the things she asked me to try to do is to forgive Sheri.

I immediately had a visceral reaction and said there was no way I could do that because there's too much hurt and pain in the way.

She's hurt me so bad, Lord, and so deeply, and in so many ways that it seems unimaginable for me to forgive her.

In the meantime, I've been so chained and so entangled in the nets and so tormented, and I've been crying out to you, Lord, repeatedly, to please get this thing off me, and to please break the chains, and please cut the nets, and please set me free.

And then, quite unexpectedly, this evening I found in a drawer of the credenza behind my desk a chapter entitled *Releasing Those Who Have Hurt Us*.

So I read the chapter, Lord, and it was very powerful to me, and I think it might be an answered prayer.

The chapter focuses on a passage from your Word, Lord, where Jesus gives the parable in Matthew 18 of the king who went about the business of settling his accounts with his servants.

It's the story where the servant is forgiven by his master an enormous debt of ten thousand bags of gold, but then, after being forgiven, he turns around and refuses to forgive a fellow servant who owes him just one hundred pieces of silver.

In verses 27 & 28 of the passage, two very important words are juxtaposed against one another, and the words are "released" and "seized."

The servant was "released" by his master, but he then "seized" his fellow servant.

Dear God, I think I'm seeing that this unexpected path is the answer to my prayer.

I cannot and I will not be set free from the hurt and torment of what Sheri has done to me until I forgive her, for freedom comes through forgiveness.

I know that I, myself, have been forgiven of so much, Lord.

I have made so many huge and terrible and catastrophic mistakes in my life, and I, myself, have hurt so many people.

I am the man who owes a debt that I could never pay back.

I am the man who owes a debt of ten thousand bags of gold to his Master.

And praise be to God, I am the man who has been "released" by his Master from the debt that I could never repay.

Thank you so much, God.

But then I am also the man who has turned around to metaphorically "seize" my fellow servant, and demand that she pays for the crimes she has committed against me.

She indeed owes me a debt of one hundred pieces of silver, but the debt she owes me is nothing compared to the debt that I, myself, have been forgiven of.

So I need to forgive Sheri, Lord.

And through this act of forgiveness, I, myself, will be set free, and the chains will be broken, and the nets will be cut, for freedom comes through forgiveness.

Praise be to God.

So I'm going to work on this, Lord.

I'm going to take it very seriously.

It will be one of the single most important spiritual exercises of my life, Lord, so I want to take my time, and I want to go slow, and I want to do this right, but I already feel a wonderful sense of freedom in my heart.

I pray, oh God, that this is not just an emotional and fleeting feeling that will be gone momentarily.

I pray that it's true, Lord.

I pray for your mercies, oh God, for a true and lasting breakthrough in my heart and life.

I don't want to hold on with white knuckles, Lord.

I want genuine breakthrough and freedom from this thing that has been holding me and smothering me.

My release and freedom will come through forgiving the one who has so deeply hurt and wounded and taken from me.

I pray, oh God, for your mercies.

May I find genuine forgiveness in my heart toward Sheri for what she's done to me.

If you help me to do this, Lord, I think it will be the single most significant act of forgiveness I've ever offered another in my life, and among the most significant acts of freedom and release that I, myself, have ever experienced.

Thank you for showing me this, Lord.

Thank you for showing me the way forward.

I pray for your help, oh God, and your mercies and your strength and your power and the filling of the Holy Spirit and the fruit of the Holy Spirit that I might be able to extend this forgiveness and pardon toward the one who does not deserve it, in the same way that I, myself, do not deserve the forgiveness that's been offered to me.

Be my helper, oh God.

I confess my weaknesses and defects of character to you, Lord.

Help me to forgive Sheri, and please release me from the chains and nets that have enslaved me.

I call upon you, oh God, and I put my hope in you, oh God.

In Jesus' Name I pray.

Amen.

This was the beginning of my "journey of forgiveness." I asked God to please show me what I needed to do to forgive. I asked God to show me how to forgive, not just in my head but in my heart. I promised God that if he would show me what he wanted me to do, that I would obey him, and I would take each step that he showed me to the very best of my ability. I knew I had no other option because of how horrible the darkness and torment of the past two years of my life had been. I was desperately willing to do whatever God required of me so that he could break the chains and cut the nets that I had been enslaved to. I needed to learn to breathe again, and I needed to come back to the land of the living. I needed God to do for me what I could never do for myself, and I knew that in a mystery, forgiveness was the pathway to my own freedom.

This began the amazing, wonderful, mysterious, and redemptive "pathway of forgiveness" that I've been walking on

Chapter #6

ever since then. As God showed me each step along the pathway, I followed him forward the best I could. I would think about what God was showing me, and I would pray about it, and I would write psalms to God as I sought to obey and apply that particular principle of forgiveness to my own heart, life, and situation. As I took that step, God would then show me the next step, and then the next step, and then the next step. Along the way, I was praying about forgiveness, talking to people about forgiveness, and listening to sermons and teachings about forgiveness. I was trying to understand forgiveness, not just in my head, but in my heart and in my life, in a deeper and more real way than I ever had before. And the good news is that it really is true that *when you forgive them, it sets you free!*

As I moved slowly forward on my "journey of forgiveness," I began to experience more relief, more peace, and more acceptance than I had known for the past two years. One day, about seven weeks into my journey, I was talking to my sister on the phone. During our conversation, she told me I sounded "different." She said she could tell I was more at peace and that I sounded "chill." I sounded more at peace because I *was* more at peace. Praise be to God!

In section two of this book, I'm going to share with you the Thirteen Principles of Forgiveness that God has shown me and is helping me to understand. The Thirteen Principles are intended to be very practical and hands-on, and along the way, you're invited to apply each principle to your own heart, life, and situation in whatever way you think best. If you, like me, have been tormented by how deeply someone has hurt your heart and life, and if you need to take your own "journey of forgiveness", I encourage you to do the work you need to do, and I pray the Thirteen Principles of Forgiveness will be a blessing to you on your journey.

Part Two
The Journey of Forgiveness

Seven

God's Pathway Is Counterintuitive

"For my thoughts are not your thoughts, neither are your ways my ways," declares the Lord.
Isaiah 55:8

WARNING! WARNING! WARNING! The first steppingstone on the journey of forgiveness is that God's pathway is counterintuitive, and the word "counterintuitive" is defined as *contrary to intuition or common-sense.*

If I asked you to put your hand in a campfire, you probably wouldn't do it because it would be counterintuitive, and it wouldn't make common-sense. If I asked you to eat some broken glass or to put your fingers in a rat trap or to jab an ice pick in your eye, you wouldn't do it because all these things would be counterintuitive, and they wouldn't make sense.

In much the same way, what God says about forgiveness is counterintuitive and will probably be the exact opposite of your human proclivity and natural sensibilities.

The bible says the thoughts and the ways of God are not like our thoughts and ways (Isaiah 55:8), and it also says the natural man cannot accept the ways of God because they appear to be foolishness to him (I Corinthians 2:14). In many ways, the

Kingdom of God is upside down, inside out, backwards, and paradoxical. What appears to us to be "up" might be "down" in God's Kingdom, and what appears to be "in" might be "out." In God's Kingdom, Jesus said you're blessed if you're poor (Matthew 5:3), and you're blessed if you mourn (Matthew 5:4), and you're blessed if you're hungry and thirsty (Matthew 5:6). In God's Kingdom, you're blessed if you're persecuted and if people say all sort of evil things about you (Matthew 5:11). In God's Kingdom, if someone slaps you on the cheek you should turn the other cheek (Matthew 5:39), and if someone sues you in court to take your shirt you should also give them your coat (Matthew 5:40). In God's Kingdom, if you look at a woman with lust, you've already committed adultery with her in your heart (Matthew 5:28).

There are many examples of the inside out, upside down, backwards, and paradoxical reality of God's Kingdom throughout the bible. In II Kings 5, the great military commander Naaman was told by the prophet Elisha to go wash in the Jordan river seven times to be healed of his leprosy. This made the powerful man angry because he expected the prophet to greet him and heal him with fanfare, but when he did what the prophet told him, and he dunked himself in the Jordan river seven times, he was healed of his leprosy. In Judges 7, Gideon was sent with only three-hundred soldiers to fight a Midianite army of one-hundred and thirty-five thousand men, and when they fought the battle the way God told them to fight the battle, using only the odd weapons of ram's horns, clay jars, and torches, they somehow won the battle. In I Samuel 17, a boy named David fought an experienced Philistine warrior named Goliath, and all he had to fight with was a sling and a stone, and somehow the boy David defeated the Philistine giant. God spoke to Moses through a burning bush, spoke to Joseph through dreams, and spoke to Balaam through a donkey. Jesus healed a blind man by spitting in the dirt to make mud and by rubbing the mud on the blind man's eyes. All these things are counterintuitive and don't make sense to our natural under-standing of how the world works.

But God's Kingdom is radically different from this world, and another significant example of the upside down, inside out, backwards, and paradoxical Kingdom of God is what God says about forgiveness, and therefore the journey of forgiveness begins with a warning: *God's pathway is counterintuitive.*

When I understood that if I was going to do forgiveness God's way, and that I would be required to do some things that didn't even make sense to me, I wrote the following psalm concerning God's counterintuitive way of forgiveness.

Psalm 524 – Counterintuitive

Dear God,

Your way, oh God, and your Kingdom are counterintuitive.

Your way is contrary to my natural mind and intuition.

Your Kingdom is upside down, inside out, backwards, and par-adoxical.

In your Kingdom, what's up is down and what's down is up.

What's in is out and what's out is in.

Your thoughts, oh God, and your ways are often the exact op-posite of what my natural mind would think and do.

The first steppingstone on the journey of forgiveness is that God's pathway is counterintuitive.

Are you willing to consider what God says even if it seems upside down, inside out, backwards, and paradoxical?

And in the way of a metaphor, I'm reminded of a scene from the Indiana Jones movie when he's going through the cave to find the Holy Grail, and he comes go the chasm and has to walk the invisible bridge.

He remembers it's a "leap of faith," so he steps off the ledge into midair, and somehow the invisible bridge appears under his feet, and he's able to walk across the chasm.

When every single fiber of his natural mind was screaming at him that he couldn't cross the chasm, and that he'd fall to his death if he tried to do so, he exercised his faith and the invisible bridge appeared.

He had to act in direct opposition of his natural mind.

What he did was very counterintuitive.

And that's what I'm learning about forgiveness, Lord.

It's very counterintuitive.

It's an upside down, inside out, backwards, and paradoxical expression of your Kingdom.

How in the world and why in the world would I want to forgive a person who has deeply and profoundly hurt me?

How in the world and why in the world would I forgive a person who traumatized my heart and life, and then blames me for what she did?

But I see that in your Kingdom, oh God, I need to take the leap of faith into forgiveness for you to break the chains and cut the nets that have held me captive in pain and torment.

I need to take the leap of faith for the invisible bridge to appear under my feet.

It's counterintuitive, Lord.

It's the exact opposite of what my common sense would tell me to do.

"There's no way I'm going to forgive her after what she's done to me."

But that's exactly what I need to do, Lord.

This is the greatest and deepest expression and experience of forgiveness I've ever had to offer another person in my life.

The person I've loved the most in my life, and the person who has hurt me the most in my life, is the person I need to most offer the counterintuitive gift of forgiveness.

I understand, Lord, that forgiveness is not an expression of my emotion as much as it is an expression of my will.

I must choose to forgive because it's the right thing to do, Lord, and because it's the way of your Kingdom.

So I choose to forgive.

I forgive Sheri because I, myself, so desperately need forgiveness.

I forgive her, Lord, and I bless her, and I release her to you, Lord, in Jesus' Name.

Empower me, oh God, by thy precious Holy Spirit, to step off the ledge into midair, to walk in obedience across the bridge of forgiveness to the other side.

And I pray, oh God, that you will change my heart as you move the truth of forgiveness from my head down into my heart so I'm not just forgiving with my head, but I'm also forgiving from my heart.

I acknowledge my need for you, oh God, and I bless your Holy Name.

In Jesus' Name I pray.

Amen.

If you're like me, forgiveness is not easy for you to offer because it's very counterintuitive, and it doesn't make sense. It's upside down, inside out, backwards, and paradoxical. But if you're like me, you've also struggled deeply with resentment, bitterness, animosity, torment, and thoughts of vengeance because of your inability to forgive. Maybe you've had your own green monster trying to smother you and drown you.

I was recently sharing with a group of men about forgiveness when I noticed tears streaming down a man's face. I asked him what was going on, and he said he hadn't been able to forgive some people who deeply hurt him over thirty years ago. Thirty years! What God says about forgiveness might sound pretty crazy, but are you willing to consider what God says even if it seems upside down, inside out, backwards, and paradoxical?

> *The first principle of forgiveness is this:*
> God's way of forgiveness is counterintuitive.

I must choose to forgive because it's the right thing to do, Lord, and because it's the way of your Kingdom.

Eight

Key Bible Passages on Forgiveness

He replied, "Blessed rather are those who
hear the word of God and obey it.
Luke 11:28

God impressed upon my heart that I should do a study of the key passages in the bible that speak about forgiveness. It seems to make sense, after all, that if I'm interested in doing forgiveness the way God says to do forgiveness that I should seek to understand what God has to say about forgiveness. I, therefore, did an extended study on the primary passages in the bible concerning forgiveness, and I offer eight of those key passages to follow, and although there is so much that can be said about each passage, I will share only one brief observation from each one in this chapter. Many of these scriptures will be further reflected upon in the forthcoming chapters of this book.

Please note that these are just eight of the many passages in the bible that help us to understand what God says about forgiveness. I encourage you to take your time as you read, meditate, pray over, and study each one of these passages. Please allow you heart to be marinated, saturated, inundated, and infiltrated as you contemplate and meditate upon these words of God. May God bless the reading of his Holy Word.

Matthew 18:21-35

Key observation – In this parable Jesus teaches what I believe is the "power principle of forgiveness," which is that we can forgive others because we, ourselves, have been forgiven.

> *21 Then Peter came to Jesus and asked, "Lord, how many times shall I forgive my brother or sister who sins against me? Up to seven times?" 22 Jesus answered, "I tell you, not seven times, but seventy times seven.*

> *23 "Therefore, the kingdom of heaven is like a king who wanted to settle accounts with his servants. 24 As he began the settlement, a man who owed him ten thousand bags of gold was brought to him. 25 Since he was not able to pay, the master ordered that he and his wife and his children and all that he had be sold to repay the debt.*

> *26 "At this the servant fell on his knees before him. 'Be patient with me,' he begged, 'and I will pay back everything.' 27 The servant's master took pity on him, canceled the debt, and let him go.*

> *28 "But when that servant went out, he found one of his fellow servants who owed him a hundred silver coins. He grabbed him and began to choke him. 'Pay back what you owe me!' he demanded.*

> *29 "His fellow servant fell to his knees and begged him, 'Be patient with me, and I will pay it back.'*

> *30 "But he refused. Instead, he went off and had the man thrown into prison until he could pay the debt. 31 When*

the other servants saw what had happened, they were outraged and went and told their master everything that had happened.

*32 "Then the master called the servant in. 'You wicked servant,' he said, 'I canceled all that debt of yours because you begged me to. 33 **Shouldn't you have had mercy on your fellow servant just as I had on you?'** 34 In anger his master handed him over to the jailers to be tortured, until he should pay back all he owed.*

35 "This is how my heavenly Father will treat each of you unless you forgive your brother or sister from your heart." (Matthew 18:21-35)

———————————— • ————————————

Matthew 6:9-15

Key observation – The way God forgives our sins is directly connected to the way we have forgiven the sins of others.

*9 "This, then, is how you should pray: "'Our Father in heaven, hallowed be your name, 10 your kingdom come, your will be done, on earth as it is in heaven. 11 Give us today our daily bread. 12 And forgive us our debts, as we also have forgiven our debtors. 13 And lead us not into temptation but deliver us from the evil one.' 14 **For if you forgive other people when they sin against you, your heavenly Father will also forgive you. 15 But if you do not forgive others their sins, your Father will not forgive your sins.** (Matthew 6:9-15)*

———————————— • ————————————

Luke 23:33-34

Key observation – Jesus forgave those who were harming him and sinning against him while they were still harming him and sinning against him.

> *33 When they came to the place called the Skull, they crucified him there, along with the criminals—one on his right, the other on his left. 34* **Jesus said, "Father, forgive them, for they do not know what they are doing."** *And they divided up his clothes by casting lots. (Luke 23:33-34)*

Colossians 3:13

Key observation – We should forgive others because the Lord has forgiven us.

> *Bear with each other and forgive one another if any of you has a grievance against someone.* **Forgive as the Lord forgave you.** *(Colossians 3:13)*

Ephesians 4:31-32

Key observation – We should forgive others because God has forgiven us.

> *31 Get rid of all bitterness, rage, and anger, brawling and slander, along with every form of malice. 32 Be kind and compassionate to one another,* **forgiving each other, just as in Christ God forgave you.** *(Ephesians 4:31-32)*

Luke 17:3-4

Key Observation – We should forgive the same person over and over again.

> *³ So watch yourselves.* *"If your brother or sister sins against you, rebuke them; and if they repent, forgive them.* **⁴ Even if they sin against you seven times in a day and seven times come back to you saying, 'I repent,' you must forgive them."** *(Luke 17:3-4)*

Mark 11:25

Key observation – The way God forgives my sins is affected by the way I forgive others' sins.

> *And when you stand praying, if you hold anything against anyone,* **forgive them, so that your Father in heaven may forgive you your sins."** *(Mark 11:25)*

Genesis 50:15-21

Key observation – We are not to take the place of God in dispensing vengeance against those who have sinned against us, and we should bless those who have sinned against us.

> *¹⁵ When Joseph's brothers saw that their father was dead, they said, "What if Joseph holds a grudge against us and pays us back for all the wrongs we did to him?" ¹⁶ So they*

sent word to Joseph, saying, "Your father left these instructions before he died: ¹⁷ 'This is what you are to say to Joseph: I ask you to forgive your brothers the sins and the wrongs they committed in treating you so badly.' Now please forgive the sins of the servants of the God of your father." When their message came to him, Joseph wept. ¹⁸ His brothers then came and threw themselves down before him. "We are your slaves," they said. ¹⁹ **But Joseph said to them, "Don't be afraid. Am I in the place of God? ²⁰ You intended to harm me, but God intended it for good to accomplish what is now being done, the saving of many lives. ²¹ So then, don't be afraid. I will provide for you and your children." And he reassured them and spoke kindly to them.** (Genesis 50:15-21)

———————————— • ————————————

The second principle of forgiveness is this:
I should seek to understand what God says about forgiveness.

Allow your heart to be marinated, saturated, inundated, and infiltrated as you contemplate and meditate upon these words of God.

Nine

Will Over Emotions

Be kind and compassionate to one another, forgiving
each other, just as in Christ God forgave you.
Ephesians 4:31-32

The third steppingstone on the journey of forgiveness is incredibly important, and in fact, I don't know if most of us could ever forgive if we don't understand this very important truth. *Forgiveness is an exercise and obedience of your will regardless of your emotions.* Or said another way, we don't wait to forgive until we feel like forgiving. We forgive because it's the right thing to do, regardless of what our feelings may or may not be. The fact of the matter is that, for many of us, if we waited to forgive until we *felt* like forgiving in our feelings, we probably would never forgive. I think that's at least in part why the man I referenced in chapter seven was unable to forgive some people who had deeply hurt him over thirty years before. Because he was waiting to *feel* the feelings of forgiveness in order to forgive, and since he never felt the feelings of forgiveness, he just assumed he could never forgive.

I think it's also the reason I had a kneejerk reaction of repugnant offense when CJ suggested to me that I was going to have to forgive Sheri. I felt so much hurt and so much pain and so much torment because of what Sheri had done, it seemed in-

Forgiveness is
an exercise and
obedience of your
will regardless
of your emotions.

conceivable to me that I could ever forgive her. It felt like I was way over here, and forgiveness was way over there, and in between me and forgiveness were all these gigantic and insurmountable and horrible feelings that I could never overcome. So this very important and non-negotiable truth emerges in our understanding of God's way of forgiveness, which is that forgiveness is an exercise and obedience of our will regardless of our emotions. And we, therefore, forgive by faith. We forgive by obedience. We forgive because it's the right thing to do. We forgive because it's the way of God's heart and the way of God's Kingdom. We forgive even when we don't feel like forgiving because it's the obedience of forgiving that allows God to break the chains and cut the nets that are holding us enslaved, so that we, ourselves, can be set free.

Another way to say this is that you can forgive them even while you still feel the hurt of what they did to you. A primary reason people often feel frozen in their ability to forgive is because they wrongly think that forgiving means they aren't supposed to feel their hurt any more. Since we often still feel our hurt when we, in fact, have been deeply hurt, we wrongly assume we are unable to forgive. People often think they're only allowed to feel hurt *or* forgiveness and that the two are mutually exclusive. *"If I still feel hurt, that means I haven't forgiven, and if I've forgiven, I should no longer feel the hurt."* This is why people often get "stuck" and conclude they're unable to forgive, because they still feel the hurt from the situation. But what if, in reality, hurt and forgiveness are not mutually exclusive, and what if you're actually allowed to feel and hold both within yourself at the same time? Or said another way, you can still be very hurt, and you can still forgive at the same time. What if feeling hurt is not actually *contradictory* to the process of forgiveness but is actually *complementary?* It's the reality of your deep hurt that's the very evidence of the betrayal and injustice you've endured, and it's your very hurt that serves as a continual reminder of your need to forgive. If someone cut you deeply with a knife, there would, no doubt,

be significant blood flowing from the wound, but isn't it the blood itself that affirms the reality of the deep wound you've experienced and shows you the exact place that needs to be tended to and bandaged so you can experience healing?

In the bible, it speaks of offering God the "sacrifice of praise."

Through Jesus, therefore, let us continually offer to God a sacrifice of praise—the fruit of lips that openly profess his name.
(Hebrews 13:15).

I think the concept of the "sacrifice of praise" implies something very significant. It implies that I do not *feel* like praising God at this particular time, but I should still go ahead and praise God anyway, and it's the very fact that I'm willing to praise God even when I don't feel like praising God that makes the praise a "sacrifice" at that moment. And in much the same way, I think we can offer to God the "sacrifice of forgiveness," which means we may not feel like offering the forgiveness at this particular time, but it's the very fact that we're willing to forgive even when we don't feel like it that makes the forgiveness a "sacrifice" at that moment.

And in a mystery, I'd advocate that it's really good news that forgiveness can be a *sacrifice.* It's good news that we don't have to feel like forgiving in order to forgive, because if we had to feel like forgiving before we could forgive, it would be really hard to do because we might not ever feel like forgiving. That would be outside of our reach. So I'm really thankful that God doesn't tell us we have to *feel* like forgiving. He just tells us to forgive, regardless of our feelings, and that puts forgiveness within our reach. Thank goodness we're allowed to still feel hurt, and we're allowed to forgive, both at the same time.

I wrote the following psalm concerning the will to forgive versus the emotions to forgive.

Psalm 525 – Will vs. Emotions

Dear God,

I think one of the key principles of forgiveness is that forgiveness is an exercise and expression of the will more than the emotions.

I forgive because I choose to forgive.

I forgive because it's the right thing to do.

I forgive, Lord, because you said I should forgive.

I forgive because it's the way of your Kingdom.

And I forgive because I have been forgiven.

I forgive whether my emotions feel like forgiving or not.

I forgive even while I still feel deeply hurt by what she's done to me.

I don't wait until I feel forgiveness in my heart and in my feelings.

I forgive even if I don't feel the forgiveness in me and even if I feel like I don't want to forgive her.

I forgive because forgiveness is an exercise and expression of my will over my emotions.

I forgive with or without the support of my emotions, and I trust you, Lord, to change my emotions if they need to be changed.

I trust you, Lord, to push the forgiveness from my head and my will down into my heart and my emotions and my feelings.

I do my part, Lord.

I step out in forgiveness because it's the right thing to do.

And I trust you to do your part, Lord.

I trust you to change my heart and my feelings and to bring them into alignment with my obedience to forgive.

I choose to forgive Sheri as an obedience of my will, oh God.

In Jesus' Name I pray.

Amen.

The third principle of forgiveness is this:
Forgiveness is an exercise and obedience of your will regardless of your emotions.

One of the key principles of forgiveness is that forgiveness is an exercise and expression of the will more than the emotions.

Ten

Grief

He heals the brokenhearted and binds up their wounds.
Psalm 147:3

Your ability to forgive will be directly related to your ability to grieve well. The reason for this, as we considered in the last chapter, is the reality of your pain and hurt. Imagine the following metaphor: you're at one end of a hallway, and you're incredibly thirsty. At the other end of the hallway is a fountain of refreshing water. But there's only one problem. In between you and the fountain is an impassable barrier in the middle of the hallway. The barrier consists of giant boulders, engine blocks, and heavy steel beams you could never move by yourself. There's no way for you to get around the barrier or over it or under it or through it, and, therefore, the fountain of water is essentially inaccessible to you.

It's much the same way when you've been deeply and profoundly hurt by another person. You need to forgive them, but it seems there's a barrier standing between you and forgiveness, and the barrier is the deep hurt and pain that lives in your heart because of what they did to you. No matter how hard you try, there's no way for you to get around the barrier or over it or under it or through it, and, therefore, it seems

Chapter 10

like forgiveness is not accessible to you. This is why, when CJ suggested to me that I was going to have to forgive Sheri, my immediate kneejerk reaction was rebellion against her words. I didn't even have to think about what I was saying because the words virtually leapt out of my mouth, *"There's absolutely no way in the world I can forgive Sheri because there's too much hurt, and there's too much pain."* As already mentioned in the previous chapter, it seems like my hurt and forgiveness are mutually exclusive, and, as long as I have one, I can't have the other. And since my hurt is so real and alive and powerful in my heart, like a huge barrier, it makes forgiveness seem impossible for me to achieve.

And this is exactly why grief is so important and necessary on the journey of forgiveness. Because grief allows you *to do something proper with your pain.* It allows you to take your pain someplace. It allows you to process your pain. It allows you to begin moving your pain out of the way, which then makes the possibility of forgiveness accessible to you. Grief is a mechanism of the human soul which allows you to process your pain in both a healthy and appropriate way.

Another way to say this is that forgiveness is not the equivalent of ignoring your pain and hurt. It's not the equivalent of pretending like you weren't hurt, and it's not the equivalent of denying or minimizing your hurt. Your hurt is simply too important to disrespect in such a way. It's too important and intrinsic to your own dignity and personhood. Your hurt has to be acknowledged and respected. It has to be felt, honored, and processed. To just ignore your hurt would be like learning you have a malignant tumor, and then dealing with the tumor by not dealing with the tumor. This strategy would be very misguided and ill-advised. You can't deal with a malignant tumor by just ignoring it or pretending like it isn't there, and you have to deal with a tumor by dealing with the tumor. And this is the healing and redemptive value of grief. Grief provides a mechanism that allows you to face your pain, to

Your ability to forgive will be directly related to your ability to grieve well.

acknowledge it, to respect it, to feel it, and to process it. This is the equivalent of moving the giant boulders, engine blocks, and steel beams from the middle of the hallway, which then creates the possibility of you moving forward toward authentic forgiveness.

Of course, the topic of grief is worthy of an entire book all by itself, and I certainly do not claim to be an expert on grief. I don't think I'm a very good griever, just like I don't think I'm a very good forgiver. But I'm learning about both, and as a result, both my heart and my life are slowly being healed. But here are just eight basic observations to be considered about grief. Please note that these observations are taken from a previous book I wrote entitled, *God's Healing Path*.

1. Give yourself permission to grieve.

Don't try to deny your pain and hurt. Don't try to pretend like it isn't there. Don't try to pretend like what happened didn't happen. Don't try to minimize it or candy-coat it. Give yourself permission to grieve.

2. Allow yourself to begin to feel the ache of your heart and life.

Don't be so afraid of your pain. Realize that God's healing path will take you *through* your pain and hurt and not around them. You can no longer deal with your pain by not dealing with your pain. You need to give yourself permission to begin to feel the ache of both your heart and life.

3. Research grief.

Study grief. Google it. Read articles about it and watch YouTube videos. Read books about grief. Write about it and pray about it. Talk to a trusted friend or a counselor or a spiritual advisor about grief. Realize that grief is an appropriate and necessary steppingstone on your healing journey and begin your journey of grief because, as you process your pain through grief, forgiving them becomes a real possibility.

4. Don't expect to be good at grief.

In the same way most of us would be horrible at speaking Chinese if we attempted to learn the language, grief concerns the language of the heart, and learning to grieve is, therefore, similar to learning a new language. You'll likely feel uncomfortable trying to grieve and feel like you're not doing it right. That's alright. Just do your best and keep moving forward in the process to the best of your ability. Like anything else you're trying to learn, you might not be very good at it at first, but the more you do it the better you'll get, so give yourself the chance to learn how to grieve.

5. Don't let the fear of the unknown stop your process of grief.

Grief can be challenging because it's a journey into the unknown. Most of us like having a sense of control in our life, and, therefore, grief can be intimidating because we can't always see where it's taking us. Grief can feel dangerous because it feels scary to let yourself really feel the weight of the hurt and pain. Although the pathway of grief might be odd, unfamiliar, and even scary, be assured that the rewards of the journey are well worth the risk.

6. Healthy grief means no time limits.

Grief is a process that cannot be reduced to a formula to be applied in every situation. Be patient with yourself, and don't

Grief is a mechanism of the human soul which allows you to process your pain in both a healthy and appropriate way.

rush the process because rushing will tempt you to begin taking shortcuts by denying what's really happening in your heart. In my own life, I had grieved the loss of my grandson, Nino, for a prolonged period of time, and, although I thought of him on occasion, I had not felt particularly emotional for some time about his tragic death or our family's great loss. Then one evening at dinner, his name came up, and I suddenly – and unexpectedly – felt an uncontrollable and powerful wave of sadness sweep over me, and I began to cry. I was surprised – and embarrassed – that such a powerful surge of emotions could show up so unexpectedly. I was caught completely off-guard. The point is this: grief often has a will of its own and is virtually impossible to tame. Take your time; do not rush, and let the ebb and flow of grief unfold in your soul however it needs to unfold and for as long as needed. When an unexpected wave of grief comes crashing upon the shores of your heart, it only proves your heart isn't finished processing something it still needs to process. Don't resist it; don't fight it – embrace it, invite it, and cooperate with it.

7. Grief will involve many different emotions.

In the same way a diamond has many different facets that reflect the light, there are many different feelings that can reflect the complexity of grief. In 1969, Elizabeth Kubler-Ross introduced what are commonly known as the five stages of grief in her book, *On Death and Dying.* Those stages are denial, anger, bargaining, depression, and acceptance. Understand that grief is not a neat, clean, or tidy process, and it can be very messy. People who are grieving will likely transition through different emotions at different times as they process their experience: denial, shock, hurt, confusion, sadness, despondency, depression, anger, rage, and acceptance, among others. When you grieve, it's important to let yourself experience and express each of these emotions as they arise in your soul. The unpredictable roller coaster ride of grief doesn't mean you're crazy. It just means you're human. So don't be surprised if one day you feel deeply despondent. Another day, all you can do is cry, and another day, all you can do is rage. Give yourself the gift of time, and don't be surprised at the many "facets" of emotion you're likely to experience.

8. The intensity of grief will subside.

While in the bowels of grief, you may feel like you're being swallowed alive by darkness and despair, never to rise again. You may feel like all hope is lost – like you're locked in a dungeon with no windows or doors and no way of escape. But even in the traditional Kubler-Ross model of grief, *acceptance* is the final stage. There *will* be relief. There *will* be light at the end of the tunnel. You *will* be able to breathe again. Your grief will come to the place where it will be enough – not in the sense that it will be completely satisfied or finished – but in the sense that its fierce and suffocating intensity will subside. There will come a time when you've grieved enough to talk about your loved one again without a stabbing sense of loss. Enough to find yourself laughing with a friend. Enough to look forward to your next trip. Enough to enjoy a fine meal and a glass of wine. Or enough to take up a new hobby. Hold on tight and rest assured the intensity of your grief will subside.

Grieving is the fourth steppingstone on the journey of forgiveness, and it will allow you to move forward because it provides a healthy way for you to process the pain and hurt that's standing between you and your ability to forgive. I wrote the following Psalm on March 5th, 2023, which was the night before I learned about my wife and her new boyfriend.

Psalm 489– I'm So Sad Tonight

Dear God,

I'm so sad tonight, Lord.

I feel it so heavy.

I feel smothered.

It's Sunday night, after a great intensive this weekend.

I don't know if it's the letdown at the end of what's been a long, emotional weekend.

I feel like it was a great weekend, and I feel like the intensive was a great success, and maybe even lifechanging for the men who attended.

Maybe it's like Jonah being depressed after the great revival in Nineveh.

Or maybe it's like Elijah being depressed after the great victory on Mount Carmel.

There's just so many painful things happening in my life, Lord.

My son Andy won't talk to me, and I'm not allowed to see my grandchildren Eva and Luca.

My shoulder hurts me, Lord, and I have to wait for the surgery.

My hip hurts me.

My abdomen hurts me.

I have to move out of the house I've loved for over twenty years.

My life is being chopped in half financially.

And worst of all, my wife has left me and is divorcing me.

Please help me, Lord.

Please be my strength, oh God.

Sometimes it just feels so hard to go on, and I wonder if I should.

Would everyone be so much better if I was gone, Lord?

People who were my life have decided they're better off without me.

They don't want me in their life.

They want their life without me.

Does that mean I'm no good, Lord?

I just feel so sad tonight, Lord.

It feels very heavy, and it feels hard to breathe.

Please be my helper, oh God.

In Jesus' Name I pray.

Amen.

> *The fourth principle of forgiveness is this:*
> Your ability to forgive will be directly related to your ability to grieve the hurt and pain you've suffered.

Your grief will come to the place where it will be enough – not in the sense that it will be completely satisfied or finished – but in the sense that its fierce and suffocating intensity will subside.

Eleven
The Power Principle of Forgiveness

Shouldn't you have had mercy on your fellow
servant just as I had on you?
Matthew 18:33

The fifth steppingstone on the journey of forgiveness is what I believe to be the "power principle of forgiveness," which is this: you can forgive others when you realize how much you, yourself, have been forgiven. This truth is affirmed in numerus passages in the bible, including Matthew 6:9-15, Ephesians 4:31-32, Colossians 3:13, and it's the main point Jesus makes in Matthew 18:21-35 when the servant who had been forgiven a debt of ten thousand bags of gold refused to forgive a fellow servant a debt of only one hundred pieces of silver. In view of this, we see that he who begged for mercy and received mercy was unwilling to offer mercy to another, and he who begged for forgiveness and received forgiveness was unwilling to offer forgiveness to another.

The way the passage is translated in the New American Standard Bible is noteworthy because two important words are juxtaposed against one another, and they're the words "released" and "seized." The servant was "released" from his debt of ten thousand bags of gold but then "seized" his fellow ser-

When we truly begin to see and comprehend our own sin and how much we need to be forgiven of and how much we have been forgiven for, it creates a frame of reference that positions us toward the possibility of forgiving others who have hurt us.

vant who owed him one hundred pieces of silver. Apparently, in the economy of this servant's head and heart, what goes around *doesn't* come around.

Imagine if you owed me one thousand dollars. If I was myopically focused on just that one thousand dollars, it would probably seem like a really big debt , and I might say, *"That's a lot of money you owe me. One thousand dollars! I want the money you owe me, and I demand that you pay me back!"* But then, if I, myself, owed someone one million dollars, and my debt of one million was set next to your debt of one thousand, and I could see both at the same time, it would create a completely new frame of reference, which would inform me and make the debt you owe me seem really small compared to the debt that I, myself, owe. As long as I'm looking at what you owe me, it seems like a mountain, but when I set what you owe me against what I owe, my debt becomes the mountain, and your debt becomes a molehill in comparison.

And, by the way, I think maybe this was the very point Jesus was making in the Sermon on the Mount when he said,

> *"Why do you look at the speck of sawdust in your brother's eye and pay no attention to the plank in your own eye? How can you say to your brother, 'Let me take the speck out of your eye,' when all the time there is a plank in your own eye? You hypocrite, first take the plank out of your own eye, and then you will see clearly to remove the speck from your brother's eye."* (Matthew 7:3-5)

When we truly begin to see and comprehend our own sin and how much we need to be forgiven of and how much we have been forgiven for, it creates a frame of reference that positions us toward the possibility of forgiving others who have hurt us.

In view of the power principle of forgiveness, I wrote the following psalm. I share a redacted version of it here.

Chapter #11

Psalm 506 – The Power Principle of Forgiveness

Dear God,

I've been deeply ensnared by the situation with my wife's divorce.

She left me on July 6th, 2021, (six-hundred and eighteen days ago today) and it has absolutely been the worst time of my entire life ever since then.

And then, to add insult to injury, I learned just eleven days ago that Sheri was on a date with another man and was seen kissing this man.

When I learned this information, Lord, it was like a knife in my heart, among the deepest stabs I've ever felt in my life.

And since then, I've struggled very deeply with this and have even been tormented by it at various times.

Last Friday was an especially terrible day.

I felt the darkness closing in on me in such a horrible and suffocating way.

I've been pleading with you, Lord, to please help me with this and asking you to break the invisible chains that are somehow holding me enslaved to Sheri and to cut the nets I've been entangled in concerning Sheri and her divorce.

Last night, I saw the metaphor of the man in deep water who is wrapped in heavy balls and chains, and he's fighting and fighting and thrashing to keep his face above the water, but he's losing the fight, and he's being pulled under by the weights he's ensnared in.

I am that man, Lord, and I'm seeing that the heavy balls and chains that have been wrapped around me, that are tormenting me and pulling me under the deep water to suffocate me, are not just the multitude of hurts and sins and offenses and injustices that Sheri has perpetrated against me but are more significantly my own resentment, animosity, hatred, bitterness, desire for vengeance, and such.

Or, said another way, Sheri did not wrap these balls and chains around me, but I, myself, have wrapped these balls and chains around me, or at least I've allowed them to be wrapped all around me, as I've allowed what Sheri's done to me to expose and provoke the dark and poisonous proclivities of my own sinful self.

What Sheri has done to me, Lord, is so wrong in so many ways, and what she's done is not excusable, but what I've done to myself as a result of what she's done to me is even more hurtful to me than what she has done to me.

Or, said another way, Sheri is not my worst enemy, and in fact, I am my own worst enemy, and I don't need to be set free from Sheri as much as I need to be set free from myself.

So this is what I'm working on, Lord, and I pray for your mercies, oh God, that you will show me the path forward and enable and empower me to do the work that I need to do in a way that is right and honorable and pleasing to you, oh God.

I understand that I, myself, am in desperate need of forgiveness.

I understand that what I need to be forgiven of is far more terrible and ugly and egregious and heinous than the sins Sheri has committed against me.

(Please note the word "egregious" is defined as "outstandingly bad and shocking.")

She needs forgiveness, Lord, because what she's done is terrible, but I need forgiveness even more because what I've done in my life is even more terrible.

So I have no right, Lord, to demand that Sheri pay her debt to me when I, myself, have been forgiven such a greater debt.

I have no right to demand that she pay me the one hundred pieces of silver she owes me when I, myself, have been forgiven ten thousand bags of gold.

I have no right to "seize" her when I, myself, have been "released."

So I'm seeking to truly forgive Sheri from the deepest place of my heart, Lord.

I do not want the forgiveness I offer her to be superficial, Lord, but genuine and sincere.

I do not want the forgiveness I offer her to be from my head but truly from my heart, for Jesus said, "*This is how my heavenly Father will treat each of you unless you forgive your brother or sister from your heart.*"

And I want to be forgiven, Lord, and I need to be forgiven.

So I pray to you, oh God, that you help me to truly embrace this act of forgiveness from my heart.

And I understand, oh God, and I'm trusting in you, oh God, that as I do this, you will do for me something I cannot do for myself, and you will break the heavy balls and chains off of my heart and soul, and you will cut the nets that I've been entangled in, and you will set me free, Lord.

So I'm asking you, Lord, first to help me see with clarity what I, myself, am in need of forgiveness for and how great the debt is that I need to be forgiven of because that will enable me to see the ten thousand bags of gold I've been forgiven of, which will empower me to forgive Sheri for the one hundred silver coins she owes me.

I'm pleading with you, as the servant pleaded with his master, to have mercy upon me and to forgive me my debts and then to help me, according to the words of Jesus, "to forgive those who have trespassed against me."

And I do know, Lord, and I give you my thanks and my praise that you have indeed forgiven my sins and washed me clean by the blood of my Savior, Jesus.

Praise be to God, and thanks be to God.

Hear my cries this day for your mercy, oh God.

In Jesus' Name I pray.

Amen.

> *The fifth principle of forgiveness is this:*
> You can forgive others when you realize how much you
> yourself have been forgiven.

The power principle of forgiveness is this: you can forgive others when you realize how much you yourself have been forgiven.

Twelve
Forgive Me My Debts

And forgive us our debts, as we also have forgiven our debtors.
Matthew 6:12

As I was attempting to follow God on the journey of forgiveness he was revealing to me, and when I understood the "power principle of forgiveness," which is that you can forgive others when you realize how much you yourself have been forgiven, I felt a very strong conviction from God that he wanted me to start by looking *at my own sins.* As the old saying states, you shouldn't put the cart before the horse, and in this sense, I could discern the Lord wanted me to focus on Tony's sins before I focused on any of Sheri's sins. In the verbiage of the parable of the unforgiving servant, I felt very strongly that God wanted me to start by focusing on the ten thousand bags of gold I had been forgiven of instead of the one hundred pieces of silver that Sheri owed me. Instead of glancing at the pile of my own sins, and then staring at the pile of Sheri's sins, I knew the Lord was requiring me to seriously focus upon and to contemplate the ten thousand bags of gold that I had been forgiven of. I knew God was asking me, not just to glance at my sins or minimize or justify or rationalize or candy coat my own sins, but to do a serious inventory of my very own defects of character, faults, shortcomings, failures, and sins.

I thought to myself, *"Tony, God wants you to take a serious look at yourself. You need to look in the mirror and see who you are. Don't just take a peek or a glimpse or a fleeting look at the many sins and failures of your life as you quickly pass them by, but instead, take a stop so you can visit them for a while. Walk around your sins, Tony. Walk through your sins, almost as if you're visiting and browsing your way through the various displays at a museum. Climb the mountain of your sins. Dig through your sins. Remember your sins, Tony. Reflect upon how much you have been forgiven of. Reflect upon how much you've needed mercy in your life. Reflect upon how deeply and profoundly you've harmed and hurt so many people in your life. Reflect upon how desperately you've needed forgiveness from so many people that you've deeply hurt by sinning against them."*

So this is what I did, not so much because it was something I really wanted to do, but because I knew it was something the Lord was requiring of me. I intended to write a psalm focusing on Sheri's many sins against me, but I knew the Lord first wanted me to write a psalm focusing on my many sins. In the verbiage of the Lord's prayer, I knew God wanted me to comprehend the many debts I'd been forgiven of, which could then position my heart toward the possibility of me forgiving my debtors as I had been forgiven.

And let me say this wasn't really a very pleasant spiritual exercise and was, in reality, quite difficult. As I browsed my way through "The Museum of Tony's Sins and Failures," the museum turned out to be way bigger than I realized. It was like when you visit a major attraction, like when Sheri and I went to The Smithsonian Institution in Washington DC, and you realize there's no way you can see this entire thing, even if you were to spend several days there. As I walked among the various displays and exhibits of Tony's sins, I saw so many things that were so ugly and so terrible. I could smell things that smelled rotten, odious, putrid, and foul. I could taste things that were unpleasant, horrible, rancid, and bitter. There were things that were so ugly, things that were hideous, things that were repulsive, and things that were heinous. I saw what I did here, and I saw what I did there. I heard what I said here, and I heard what I said there. I remembered what I did to this person and what I did to that person. I remembered how I was so selfish here, and when I demanded my way there. I remembered when I took from that person to serve my own selfish or lust-filled passions, and I remembered when I took from that other person. There was selfishness, pride, hatred, lust, fornication, adultery, greed, and murder in my heart. And there was bitterness and unkindness, cruelty and rage, jealousy and idolatry. On and on it went, and I realized I probably could never truly fathom the depths of my own sinful heart.

I understand the Puritans of old would pray to God for what they called "the gift of tears." They would pray that God would help them to truly see the depths of their sin and then give them the ability to weep over their sin. I think it's a really good prayer to pray, and it's exactly what David said when he prayed to God,

Search me, O God, and know my heart: try me, and know my thoughts: And see if there be any wicked way in me, and lead me in the way everlasting.
(Psalm 139:23-24).

It's a good prayer to pray, but be careful because when you pray this prayer, God might just give you the answer.

I wrote the following psalm to God entitled *Ten Thousand Bags of Gold*, and I share a redacted version of it here. Please note that while I'm sharing both the introduction and the conclusion of the psalm here, I'm not sharing the main body of the psalm, in which I wrote out a list enumerating at least one-hundred and thirty-one different failures and sins of my life, including reflections on many of the people I've harmed through my sins.

I knew God was asking me, not just to glance at my sins or minimize or justify or rationalize or candy coat my own sins, but to do a serious inventory of my very own defects of character, faults, shortcomings, failures, and sins.

Psalm 507 – Ten Thousand Bags of Gold

Dear God,

I'm a deeply broken man.

I'm a sinner, Lord.

I don't only commit sins, but I have an even deeper problem because I'm a sinner. A spider's problem isn't just that he makes spider webs. His problem is that he's a spider, and that's why he makes spider webs.

My sin is not just what I do, Lord, but it's who I am.

I have a heart of independence and autonomy and defiance and mutiny and rebellion against you, God, and against your rightful place of supreme authority in my heart and life.

I'm guilty as Adam and Eve were guilty in the Garden of Eden.

They disobeyed you, Lord.

They acted in clear defiance of your simple instructions, as I have also done in many different ways.

There's a law of sin within me, Lord, that continuously compels me to do what I want to do, even when I know it's in defiance of you, Lord, and defiance of your Kingdom.

It's really quite terrible, Lord, and you might think I'd have this struggle figured out better than I do after knowing you for fifty years now.

So I confess my sins to you, oh God.

Or at least I will mention a brief list of outstanding sins as they occur to me, but I acknowledge, Lord, that my sins are far greater than I could ever enumerate if I were to write ten thousand pages of my sins.

I acknowledge to you, Lord, that there must be so many sins deep within me that I do not even see or consciously understand.

Only you can see the depths of my heart, Lord.

You know me like I don't even know myself, and you know my sins even more than I do.

You know the thoughts and intents and motives of my heart, Lord, even when I do not.

You see me even when I can't see me.

But I will do my best to confess my sins to you, oh God, and I'm asking for your help, and for your forgiveness through Christ.

Where oh where do I begin, and how do I even begin to name the sins of my life?

(Enumeration of at least one-hundred and thirty-one failures and sins of my life here.)

I confess that I have...

I confess that I have...

I confess that I have...

I confess that I have...

I've written about my sins for seven pages now, and I know that so much more could be written.

Maybe this is enough for now, Lord.

Maybe it's enough to establish the primary point toward my purpose here, to bring into focus the ten thousand bags of gold I owe, which creates a frame of reference that informs and balances the one hundred pieces of silver that Sheri owes me.

I must see my own sins, oh God, in order to forgive Sheri's sins against me.

I must see how much I, myself, need forgiveness in order to extend forgiveness to Sheri.

I must see how much I, myself, need mercy in order to extend mercy to Sheri.

I want to forgive her from my heart, oh God.

I want to be set free from the heavy balls and chains that I have wrapped around my own soul.

I pray, oh God, that you will set me free.

I'm so sorry, Lord, for my many, many sins.

I'm so sorry, Lord, for the way I've hurt you and hurt so many people.

I'm so sorry for my autonomy and rebellion against you.

I'm so sorry that Jesus had the weight of all my sins upon him on the cross, in addition to all the sins of the world that were placed upon him already.

Please forgive me, oh God.

Please cleanse me of my many, many sins.

Please help me to see my many sins, oh God, so I may forgive those who have sinned against me.

In Jesus' Name I pray.

Amen.

The sixth principle of forgiveness is this: I should do a comprehensive inventory of my own sins and defects of character to realize how much I myself need forgiveness.

I must see how much I myself need forgiveness in order to extend forgiveness to Sheri.

The seventh steppingstone on the pathway of forgiveness is to actually forgive the person you need to forgive.

Thirteen

Forgiving Them

*For if you forgive other people when they sin against you,
your heavenly Father will also forgive you.*
Matthew 6:14

The seventh steppingstone on the pathway of forgiveness is to
actually forgive the person you need to forgive. At this point
on my journey, I felt led to write a psalm *to God* to announce
and proclaim and articulate my actual confession of forgiveness for the many hurts, offenses, sins, and violations of relationship that Sheri had perpetrated against me. I was articu-
lating my confession of forgiveness, not to Sheri, but to God.
Please note that later in the journey of forgiveness, I was led
to write a confession of forgiveness, not to God, but to Sheri
herself (Chapter seventeen). But at this point, I was talking to
God about my forgiveness of Sheri.

You might think that if the goal is to forgive another person,
that you would start at step one by just forgiving that person,
but I think it's noteworthy to observe that this was actually the
seventh steppingstone on the journey of forgiveness on which
God was leading me. This means there were six steppingstones I had to recognize, understand, and work on before I
was truly ready to express my actual confession of forgiveness

toward Sheri. It's kind of like when you build a house; you put the foundation in first, and then you build the actual house upon that foundation. In much the same way, we need to do the work and put in place a strong foundation upon which we can then enact the actual forgiveness that we're offering the person who has hurt us. In the same way a house built upon the sand will almost surely fall down when the storms come, forgiveness that's offered too quickly with little to no foundation will likely collapse when the integrity of that forgiveness is tested by the strain of the work that's necessary to maintain the forgiveness over time. (Please note that we'll consider the "work of forgiveness" in the next chapter.)

In the way of a quick review, let's look at the six foundational steppingstones that precede the actual confession and act of forgiveness itself so we understand what will prepare us to truly forgive. We need to...

1. Understand that God's pathway is counterintuitive.

2. Understand what God says about forgiveness through the key bible passages on forgiveness.

3. Understand that forgiveness is an expression of the will over the emotions.

4. Understand the importance of grief on the journey of forgiveness.

5. Understand "the power principle of forgiveness," which is that we can forgive others when we realize how much we have been forgiven.

6. Understand how much we need forgiveness by doing an honest assessment and inventory of our own failures and sins.

These six foundational steppingstones are critically important in preparation for the act of forgiveness itself, and because the Lord had helped me understand and process these six steppingstones first, I was now ready to express and articulate to God my actual confession of forgiveness toward Sheri.

The other noteworthy observation I'll share here is that it's important to specifically name the actual hurts, offenses, and sins for which you're offering forgiveness, as opposed to a vague or generic statement of forgiveness. *"I forgive Bob for stealing my tools, and for then getting angry at me and threatening me when I asked for my tools back"* is better than just *"I forgive Bob."* In fact, I'd suggest that naming specific offenses and violations of relationship is both appropriate and necessary in both directions of forgiveness. Not only when you're forgiving another person (*"I forgive you specifically for..."*), but also when you're the one asking for forgiveness (*"Will you forgive me specifically for..."*).

Many years ago, a dear and trusted friend of mine deeply hurt both me and our friendship through a significant betrayal. Our relationship was not the same thereafter, and several years later, he reached out to me, which I appreciated, in the attempt to ask for my forgiveness. We met for lunch, but the best he could offer was a very vague apology that didn't really acknowledge any details whatsoever or take any responsibility for his specific sins against me. *"I'm sorry if I hurt you or offended you"* isn't a very satisfying apology by itself because it doesn't even acknowledge or name what the hurtful or offensive action was to begin with, and at the very best, it's like a half of an apology, because the person is offering an apology without even identifying what it is that they're apologizing for.

In response I asked him, *"What specifically are you sorry for?"* and he essentially stammered around and was unable to name anything even approximating the actual violations of relationship he had perpetrated against me. It was so disap-

It's important to specifically name the offenses you're asking for forgiving, for if you're the one asking for forgiveness, and to specifically name the offenses you're forgiving if you're the one doing the forgiving.

pointing. We learn, therefore, that it's important to name the offenses you're asking forgiveness for, if you're the one asking for forgiveness, and to specifically name the offenses you're forgiving, if you're the one doing the forgiving. In this way, if you're the one asking for forgiveness, you know exactly what you're being forgiven for, and if you're the one offering the forgiveness, you know exactly what you're forgiving.

I wrote the following psalm to God as a confession of my forgiveness for the hurts, offenses, sins, and violations of relationship that Sheri had perpetrated against me. Please note that this is a redacted version of the psalm. I'm sharing here both the introduction and the conclusion of the psalm, but I have omitted the main body of the psalm where I named at least ninety-one specific offenses and sins through which Sheri had deeply harmed both my heart and my life.

Psalm 509 – Forgiving Sheri's One Hundred Pieces of Silver

Dear God,

I understand I need to forgive Sheri for what she's done to me.

She's hurt me and harmed my life more deeply than any person has ever hurt me.

I need to forgive her for all the hurt and pain and suffering and anguish and torment and trauma that she's caused my heart and life.

I understand, Lord, that forgiveness is the right thing for me to do.

I understand that forgiveness is the way of your heart, mind, will, purpose, and Kingdom, oh God.

In the Lord's prayer, Jesus taught us to pray, "And forgive us our debts, as we forgive our debtors." (Matthew 6:12)

I want you to forgive me, Lord, so I need to forgive my debtors.

So I pray, oh God, that you will witness and receive and bless the forgiveness I'm offering to Sheri for her many offenses against me.

I pray for the blood of Jesus over this sacrifice of forgiveness.

I pray, oh God, that as I offer Sheri my forgiveness, it will not just be an exercise of my head but an exercise of my heart.

I pray that as I speak these words of forgiveness, Lord, in obedience to you, that you will cause the words to transition and to metamorphose from my head into my heart.

I recently reflected on my own sinfulness when I wrote Psalm 507 entitled, *Ten Thousand Bags of Gold.*

I am the servant who owes a debt of ten thousand bags of gold, and therefore, how can I not forgive another who owes me a debt of just one hundred pieces of silver?

How can I be "released" from my debtor, only to "seize" upon the one who still owes me a debt?

I, therefore, do not offer my forgiveness to Sheri from a place of pride and self-righteousness.

I'm not saying that I'm better than her, Lord, and quite to the contrary, I'm acknowledging that I have committed far more sins in my life for which I need forgiveness than Sheri has committed against me.

I also recognize, Lord, that I have failed Sheri in many ways, and I have sinned against her, and I have harmed her in many ways.

So I need both your forgiveness, Lord, and her forgiveness.

But the purpose of this psalm is not to focus on my sins against Sheri but to focus on my forgiveness of Sheri for her sins against me.

In the shadow of Matthew 18, in the parable of the unforgiving servant, there's a very real sense in which my sins are far greater than Sheri's sins, but that does not mean that her sins against me are trivial or irrelevant or insignificant.

They are very significant, and they are profound, and they have been heinous and very hurtful and very harmful and very traumatic in both my heart and my life.

Sheri has hurt me far more than any other person has ever hurt me in my entire life.

Nobody else is even close, Lord.

But I'm asking you for something, Lord.

I'm asking you for something that I cannot do for myself.

I'm asking you to break the chains that have been holding me in bondage to Sheri and her divorce and the nets in which I've been entangled.

I'm asking you, oh God, to set me free so I can be free indeed.

You know, Lord, that I sincerely tried to fight for our marriage, and I did everything I could possibly do to try to save our marriage.

But none of that worked, Lord, and my soon-to-be ex-wife is determined to have her divorce.

So I release my marriage to you, Lord, and I release Sheri to you, and I release our wedding vows to you, and I release our thirty-nine years of marriage to you, and I release myself to you and my heart and my future and my ministry and all that I am.

And I release all my hurt and pain and trauma to you, Lord.

And through this Psalm, I'm now releasing my forgiveness for Sheri to you.

And I'm asking you to do what only you can do, to purify my heart, oh God, and to change my heart and make these words of forgiveness be true, not just in my head but in my heart, and break the chains that have been holding me and the nets that have been holding me and set me free, Lord.

So with all that being said, I now speak these words of forgiveness over Sheri for the hurt and pain and harm and sins and trauma that she's caused my heart and life.

(Enumeration of at least ninety-one of
Sheri's failures and sins against me here.)

I forgive Sheri for...

I forgive Sheri for...

I forgive Sheri for...

I forgive Sheri for...

I speak these words of forgiveness over Sheri in Jesus' mighty Name.

I speak these words of forgiveness in the Name of the One who, Himself, is the Mighty Forgiver.

I speak these words and this heart of forgiveness as one who, himself, is in such great need of forgiveness.

And I speak these words of forgiveness by faith, oh God, and I pray that you cause these words of forgiveness to permeate and infiltrate and saturate and marinate to the very deepest depths of my heart, oh God.

I pray for the mighty and powerful blood of Jesus over this

I pray that as I speak these words of forgiveness, Lord, in obedience to you, that you will cause the words to transition and to metamorphose from my head to my heart.

confession of forgiveness and over the heart that is making this confession.

I pray, oh God, that you will receive and bless my humble and feeble attempt to extend forgiveness to the one who has so profoundly hurt and harmed my life.

I pray that these confessions of forgiveness will arise to you, oh God, like the smoldering smoke and aroma from a burnt offering sacrificed to you, and I pray that this sacrifice of forgiveness is pleasing in your sight.

I pray, oh God, that you will breathe the smoldering aroma of these confessions of forgiveness deeply within your nostrils, oh God, and I pray you might bless this sacrifice of forgiveness by the release and anointing and power of your blessing and of your Holy Spirit and of your heart and of your Kingdom.

I speak, by faith, forgiveness over Sheri in Jesus Name.

I say forgiveness, forgiveness, forgiveness, forgiveness, forgiveness.

I proclaim forgiveness, forgiveness, forgiveness, forgiveness, forgiveness.

I pray forgiveness, forgiveness, forgiveness, forgiveness, forgiveness.

I pray that this forgiveness will be embedded in my heart and in my life, oh God, like a mighty and immovable rock that is, itself, established on bedrock.

I pray this forgiveness will be forever alive and powerful in my heart, oh God, and I pray that you will break the encumbrances of any chains and any nets that exist in my heart and life.

I pray these chains and nets will be exposed by you, oh God, and renounced by you, oh God, and I pray they will dry up and shrivel up like the tree that Jesus cursed, and I pray they will fall down to the ground, forever void and powerless and impotent.

I pray, oh God, that you renounce the chains and nets from my life, Lord, in the way you renounced lameness from the lame man and blindness from the blind man and leprosy from the leper and the way you renounced death from Lazarus.

I am your servant, oh God.

I am your child.

I belong to you, oh God.

You are my Master, and you are my Lord.

I seek to move forward on this path of forgiveness by faith, oh God, and I do so with trembling and weakness, but I'm thankful, oh God, that your strength is made perfect in my weakness.

As the widow offered her two mites to God, I offer my forgiveness of Sheri to both her and to you, Lord.

I pray, oh God, that this offering and sacrifice of forgiveness is acceptable in your sight.

I pray the seeds of forgiveness that I'm planting in your Kingdom this night, oh God, might sprout and grow and grow and grow into a mighty oak of forgiveness that will cast a great shadow of your Kingdom that might somehow provide rest, shelter, and protection for many other weary travelers.

I acknowledge my great need for you, Lord, and I bless your Holy Name forevermore.

I say that you are the True and Almighty and Sovereign God,

and I say that I love you, oh God.

In Jesus's mighty Name I pray.

Amen.

The seventh principle of forgiveness is this:
I need to articulate and proclaim to God my actual statement
of forgiveness for the one who has hurt me.

I pray that this forgiveness will
be embedded in my heart and in
my life, oh God, like a mighty and
immovable rock that is, itself,
established on bedrock.

Fourteen
The Work of Forgiveness

Jesus answered, "I tell you, not seven times,
but seventy times seven."
Matthew 18:22

If you're trying to do forgiveness, the content of this chapter is incomprehensibly important to understand. It concerns the eighth steppingstone on the journey of forgiveness, which is *the work of forgiveness.* The main idea is that forgiveness is not an event but a process. Forgiveness is not "one and done" because, if you're like me, forgiveness is not easy for you to do, and you're going to have to work on it. Forgiveness is not a neat, clean, and tidy process. It's messy. It's not a linear process from Point A to Point B. It's much more erratic than that. It's unpredictable. It's volatile. It's two steps forward and one step back. And sometimes it feels like it's two steps forward and ten steps back. In short, forgiveness is not necessarily an easy thing to do, and, therefore, if we're going to have any measure of success, we're going to have to do "the work of forgiveness."

In what could arguably be the single most important passage in the entire bible on forgiveness, Peter asks Jesus an important question:

"Master, how many times do I forgive a brother or sister who hurts me? Seven?" Jesus replied, "Seven! Hardly. Try seventy times seven."
(Matthew 18:21-22 MSG).

Jesus says we should forgive another person who hurts us not seven times, but four-hundred and ninety times! And of course, the point Jesus was making here is that we should *never* stop forgiving; we should forgive over and over and over again, endlessly. And I have an observation on this passage that I think is critically important to understand. I think most people assume that what Jesus meant by four-hundred and ninety times, is that we should be willing to forgive another person four-hundred and ninety times for four-hundred and ninety *different* offenses. For example, if a person sins against me, I should forgive them for that offense. But then, if they sin against me again, I should forgive them again for the second offense, and then for a third offense, and then for a fourth offense, and so forth, up to four-hundred and ninety *different* offenses. But I don't think this is necessarily what Jesus meant when he said four-hundred and ninety times. He wasn't just saying that we should forgive four-hundred and ninety *different* offenses, but that we might need to forgive the *same offense* over and over again, up to four-hundred and ninety times! In other words, Jesus understood human nature. He knew how hard it might be for us to forgive a very hurtful offense and that we might need to forgive that same hurtful offense, not just one time, but many times over and over again.

Here's an example for the sake of clarity. I love the outdoors, and I love to hunt. My dad initiated me into the world of men when I was a boy by hunting, and it became a passion that's deeply embedded in my soul. When I'm lucky enough to get a deer, the first thing I typically do is to eviscerate the deer in order to transport it out of the woods. One of the reasons I do this is to reduce the body weight of the animal because the entrails contribute close to twenty-five percent to the overall weight. Therefore, the gut pile from a two-hundred-pound buck would weigh an estimated fifty pounds. In this metaphor, imagine that for some reason I decided to pick up this fifty-pound gut pile and hold it in my hands. It would be a nasty, slimy, smelling, and bloody mess! And it's this gut pile in my hands that represents *unforgiveness* because, when I can't forgive, I'm holding a metaphorical slimy mess that typically includes, among other such dark factors, resentment, if not hatred, animosity, bitterness, contempt, and vengeance. And how does it often go with this slimy mess of "unforgiveness" that I'm holding in my hands? I don't like it because it's slimy, messy, and stinky, and I know I need to get rid of it, and I know I need to try to forgive. So I bring the mess to Jesus, and I lay it down at his feet, and I say that I've "forgiven" the person who's hurt me. But then, maybe the very next day, I look down and realize the slimy, bloody mess of the resentment, hatred, bitterness, contempt, and vengeance is right back in my hands again. And I think to myself, *"Oh no, Tony! How did this get back in your hands? You gave this to Jesus yesterday. I don't even know when I picked it back up, but here it is again, right back in my hands."*

So I have to bring the slimy mess back to Jesus, and I have to lay it down at his feet again. But then, I turn around and a short time later, the slimy mess is back in my hands yet again. So I have to bring it back to Jesus again and again and again and again. Not just one time or two times or three times or four times. But over and over again, even up to four-hundred and ninety times according to Jesus! And it's not that I'm forgiving for a different offense each time I forgive, but I'm actually forgiving for the *same offense* that somehow keeps magically appearing back in my hands.

Chapter #14

This is the "work of forgiveness." It's watching yourself, babysitting yourself, and bringing your hurt, pain, offense, resentment, hatred, bitterness, and desire for vengeance back to the Lord, over and over again. And what this means is that you don't get to just forgive one time, but you get to forgive, and then you get to forgive again, and then you get to forgive again and again and again and again.

And I think that understanding the "work of forgiveness" should be encouraging to us because if you're struggling to forgive, it doesn't mean you're a bad person, and it doesn't mean you're a freakshow, and it doesn't mean somethings wrong with you. It just means your human, because forgiveness is hard, and sometimes forgiveness takes a lot of work, and sometimes you might have to keep forgiving over and over again, even up to four-hundred and ninety times.

In view of the reality presented in this chapter, that sometimes we need to forgive over and over again, I wrote the following psalm entitled "The Work of Forgiveness" and share a redacted version here.

It's watching yourself, babysitting yourself, and bringing your hurt, pain, offense, resentment, hatred, bitterness, and desire for vengeance back to the Lord, over and over again.

Psalm 511 – The Work of Forgiveness

Dear God,

I can see, Lord, that forgiveness is very difficult, and it takes a lot of work.

I think forgiveness is not a passive process but a very active process.

It's not a benign process but an aggressive process.

I don't think forgiveness is given easily.

I think it takes a lot of intentional effort and hard work.

It takes persistence because, so often, *unforgiveness* is like a boomerang.

You throw it away from you, but it keeps coming back.

Peter asked Jesus, *"How many times should I forgive my brother? Seven times?"*

And Jesus gave Peter what, I'm sure, was an unexpected and maybe even shocking answer:

"Not seven times, but seventy times seven."

And I think there's a reason Jesus said this, and the reason is that Jesus understands the human heart and the human condition, and Jesus knew that we would typically have to forgive over and over again for the same offense that was perpetrated against us.

And do you know what I wish, Lord?

I wish forgiveness was like a "divine magic eraser" that would just erase all the hurt and pain of the offense the very first time, and then you could just be done with it and go on with your life.

But I don't think it works that way much of the time.

I think, metaphorically, I put the offense down at your feet, Lord, through the act of forgiveness, but then I turn around and somehow the pain and the hurt and the offense and the torment are back in my hands again, and I don't even remember picking it back up.

So I have to put it back down at your feet Lord, over and over again, and this is the "work of forgiveness."

Staying engaged in the process and doing the work and laying it back down at your feet, Lord, and then laying it down at your feet again, and again and again.

And I can tell this is what I'm going to have to do with Sheri, Lord.

I finished my Psalm of Forgiveness for Sheri's one hundred-pieces of silver against me (Psalm 509), and I wrote it very sincerely and passionately, and I really want to mean it, Lord, and I really want it to be true in my heart, but I've found myself over and over again thinking about what she's done, and feeling the pain and the hurt all over again, and feeling myself being tormented because I couldn't escape the thoughts and feelings, and then feeling the ugly and dark thoughts coming back to swirl within me, Lord.

Thoughts of resentment and bitterness and a longing for vengeance that would make Sheri pay for what she's done to me, among other such thoughts and feelings.

So the thing keeps showing up in my hands, even though I had already laid it down at your feet.

And I've had to forgive Sheri over and over again for what she's done to me, as I've repeatedly said to myself, and I've said to you, *"I forgive Sheri for what she's done to me. Help me to forgive Sheri, Lord. I forgive her, Lord. I forgive Sheri. Please get this thing off me, Lord. Please help me to forgive her. I forgive Sheri."*

And I've had to fight and fight and labor and fight to stay in the place of forgiveness, Lord, and I'm not sure I'm doing a very good job, but I think I'm trying to do the work of forgiveness and trying to forgive her over and over again as Jesus said I should do.

I don't think I'm a very good forgiver, Lord.

I think my hurt and my pain and my anger and my resentment and my sense of humiliation and my torment all swirl around on the inside of me and sabotage my efforts of forgiveness.

It's as if the thoughts and feelings come back to me and erase any progress I've made and send me right back to square one, where I have to start all over again.

Please help me to be a better forgiver, Lord.

Please help me to do the work of forgiveness.

I need your mercies over my heart and my life very much, oh God.

I am desperate for your mercies over my heart and my life.

I call upon you, oh God.

In Jesus' Name I pray.

Amen.

> *The eighth principle of forgiveness is this:* I should understand that forgiveness is not an event, but a process, and I may need to forgive the person who has hurt me, over and over again.

And I think there's a reason Jesus said this, and the reason is that Jesus understands the human heart and the human condition, and Jesus knew that we would typically have to forgive over and over again for the same offense that was perpetrated against us.

Fifteen

Blessing Them

Bless those who curse you, pray for those who abuse you.
Matthew 6:28

The ninth steppingstone on the journey of forgiveness concerns *blessing* the person who has deeply hurt you and represents for me what might be the most challenging step on the entire journey of forgiveness. I almost couldn't believe it when God put this in front of me. I was working on steppingstone eight, which we considered in the previous chapter, *The Work of Forgiveness*, and while I was praying about and writing about that steppingstone, God impressed upon me the next steppingstone, which was that God wanted me to *bless* Sheri. And I tried to object. *"Are you kidding me, Lord? It's not enough that I have to forgive her for all she's done to me, but I have to bless her too?"* But God wasn't kidding me and he answered me by showing me two different metaphors.

The first one was that of a coin. A coin has two different sides—heads and tails. You can't have a coin with just one side because a coin always has two sides. I felt that God was showing me that one side of the coin is forgiveness, and the other side of the coin is blessing. And in the same way one side of a coin completes the other side of the coin, in the upside down, inside out, backwards, and paradoxical Kingdom of God, it's the act of *blessing* the one you're forgiving that actually completes the forgiveness you're offering them. It's counterintuitive, but it's the way of God's heart and the way of his Kingdom.

The second metaphor was even more impactful in helping me understand the importance of blessing your offender. In this metaphor, I saw a picture of a mathematical scale. If you picture zero right in the middle, it becomes your beginning place of reference. You can then go up from zero into the positive side of the mathematical scale, which would be plus one, plus two, plus three, plus four, and so forth, ascending upward. But you could also go down from zero into the negative side of the mathematical scale, which would be negative one, negative two, negative three, negative four, and so forth, descending downward. And with this picture fresh in my mind's eye, it's as if I heard the Lord saying to me, "*Tony, when you forgive Sheri, it's as if you're nullifying the negative side of the scale in your emotions and heart. You're neutralizing the anger and rage and bitterness and resentment and hatred and desire for vengeance. Those things are all so negative and toxic, we need to get them out of your heart through forgiveness. But even if you erase the entire negative side of the scale, you're still just back at zero, and that's not good enough, Tony. I intend much more than that for you. I want you to actually move into the positive side of the scale and the positive territory I have planned for you. And that's why I want you to bless Sheri because blessing her will move you into redemptive territory in my Kingdom.*"

And when the Lord showed me this metaphor, it helped me to understand why I needed to not just forgive Sheri, but why I also needed to bless Sheri. I had already learned the way of God is very counterintuitive, and I had also learned that obeying God is more often an act of the will than it is of the emotions, so I knew in my heart that the next steppingstone of my obedience on the journey of forgiveness was to *bless* Sheri.

In addition, it should be noted that the action of blessing Sheri did not only happen within the immaterial arena of my own head and heart, but worked itself out in at least one very specific, tangible, and significant expression of material blessing upon her life. Or, said another way, the Lord was helping me to bless Sheri, not just with my thoughts and words on the inside of me, but also with some significant material choices and actions on the outside of me.

As I processed what I was learning about blessing, I wrote the following psalm entitled, Blessings Over Sheri, and I share a redacted version of the psalm here.

Psalm 513 – Blessings Over Sheri

Dear God,

You say I should love my enemies and bless those who curse me and pray for those who are abusive to me.

You have shown me, Lord, that I need to forgive Sheri, and I'm working on that.

I've written Psalm 509, which is entitled, *Forgiving Sheri's One Hundred Pieces of Silver.*

But I'm seeing and understanding that forgiving Sheri is not enough by itself because forgiving her, at best, is only half the formula, and what you want me to do, Lord, is to go beyond forgiveness to actually *bless* her, because forgiveness is

It's the act of blessing the one you're forgiving that actually completes the forgiveness you're offering them.

the spiritual energy that allows me to process and release the negative, but blessing is the spiritual energy that allows me to process and establish the positive.

And it seems very counterintuitive to bless the person who has caused you so much hurt and pain, but that's the way of your heart, oh God, and the way of your Kingdom.

So this psalm is a psalm of blessing over Sheri.

I want this psalm to take me into the positive Kingdom territory you intend for me, Lord.

I don't just want to forgive Sheri for the hurt and pain and torment and trauma she's caused me, but I actually want to *bless* her, Lord, because that's what you told me to do.

So I want to bless Sheri, Lord, but even more than that, I want to ask you to bestow an abundance of blessings upon her, oh God.

I looked up the word "bless" in the original language, and the best I can tell, the definition of the word implies to pray and to ask and to invoke the blessings and favor of God upon another person.

So it's not that I'm the source of the blessing, Lord, as if I have any power or authority whatsoever to bless Sheri, but it's acknowledging and asking for you, who is the Almighty Blesser, to actually bestow an abundance of blessings upon Sheri in every way, for you have the power to bless her, Lord, and I do not.

So this is my psalm of blessing over Sheri.

I'm asking you, oh God, to bless Sheri's life in every way.

I'm asking you, oh God, to bestow an abundance of your blessings over her.

I pray your blessings flow over Sheri like a mighty river, oh God.

I pray that you will be her helper, oh God.

I pray that you will be her strength.

I pray that you will be her light.

I pray that you will be her wisdom, oh God.

I pray that you will be her protection.

I pray for an abundance of your favor over her life in every way, Lord.

I pray you bless her physical health and body.

I pray you bless her finances, Lord.

I pray you bless all the relationships of her life, Lord, including her family relationships, her friendships, and her relationships with our children and grandchildren.

And I pray you bless her relationship with the new man she's with, from the Rendezvous Café.

And if things don't work out with that person, I pray you bring the right man to Sheri at the right time.

I pray, oh God, that you bring her a good man with a good heart that she can enjoy a wonderful relationship with.

I pray you bless her with happiness, Lord.

I pray you bless her with joy.

I pray you bless her with an abundance of your peace, Lord.

I pray you bless her spiritual walk with you, Lord.

I pray you bless Sheri with clarity of heart and mind and soul.

I pray that you bless Sheri by leading her and guiding her on the path you have for her life, Lord.

I pray you bless her with the ability to discern your voice whispering to her.

I pray you bless her, Lord, by protecting her from the schemes of the enemy who wants to perpetrate hurt and harm and destruction upon her life.

I pray you bless Sheri to serve you, Lord.

I pray you bless Sheri to be in the center of your will for her life, Lord.

I pray you bless Sheri by smiling over her.

I pray you bless Sheri by singing over her, Lord.

I pray you bless Sheri with the breath of God upon her life.

I pray you bless Sheri with your eye upon her, Lord.

I pray you bless Sheri by hearing her prayers, Lord, and by answering her prayers.

I pray you bless Sheri by granting her the desires of her heart.

I pray you bless Sheri and make her latter years much better and sweeter than her former years.

I pray you bless Sheri from the top of her head to the tips of her toes.

I pray you bless Sheri from the inside out and from the outside in.

I pray you bless Sheri above her and below her and to the left of her and to the right of her.

I pray you bless Sheri with angels all around her.

I pray you bless all of Sheri's future plans, Lord.

I pray you bless her to sell what was our marital home, if that's what she decides to do, and I pray you bless her to find her new home.

I pray you bless her with the sun by day and the moon by night.

I pray you bless her with many smiles and much laughter.

I pray you bless Sheri by ordering her steps, Lord.

I pray you bless her by forgiving her sins, Lord.

I pray you bless Sheri with your presence, and I pray you bless her by casting your shadow over her.

I pray you bless her with eyes to see whatever you need to show her, Lord, and ears to hear your voice whispering to her.

Sheri has many defects of character, Lord, and she has hurt both my heart and my life deeply and profoundly, but she is a good person with a good heart, and I pray you bless her heart, oh God.

I pray for significant and powerful and mighty blessings of God over her life in every single way, Lord.

I speak forth in faith, and I align my heart with your heart, oh God, and I align myself in obedience to your word and your Kingdom, and I speak all these blessings over Sheri, but more than that, Lord, I pray for your Almighty blessings over her life in every single way.

I pray for your blessings, oh God, not added, but multiplied over Sheri in every single way.

I pray for an explosion of your blessings all around Sheri in every single way.

I speak and I pray for blessings, blessings, blessings, blessings, blessings, blessings, blessings, blessings, and blessings over Sheri.

And after all those blessings, Lord, I speak and pray for more blessings, blessings, blessings, blessings, blessings, blessings, blessings, and blessings over both her heart and her life in every single way.

I offer this prayer and psalm of blessings over Sheri by faith, oh God, and I pray that you cause this prayer and psalm of blessing to take root in my heart, Lord, and not just in my head.

I pray this prayer and psalm of blessing is a sweet fragrance in your nostrils, oh God, an aroma that's pleasing to you, Lord.

I say that you're the Almighty Blesser who has blessed me when I don't deserve to be blessed, and you are the Almighty Blesser who will bless the one who has so deeply hurt my heart and my life, even though she does not deserve to be blessed.

I say that I will call upon you, Lord, and I will worship you, and I will serve you, and I will live for you, and I will obey you, and I will love you, both now and forevermore.

Blessed be the Name of the Lord forevermore.

In Jesus' Name I pray.

Amen.

I'd like to conclude this chapter with an important word of testimony. As I slowly worked my way along the journey of forgiveness God was showing me, steppingstones one through eight, not much was really changing in my heart or my emotions, and I was still struggling significantly with the dark thoughts and feelings and the sense of torment and the green beast that was still trying to suffocate me. But when I finally made it to steppingstone nine, which is the stepping-stone of *blessing*, and I wrote my psalm of blessing over Sheri, I began to experience, for the first time, in my heart and my emotions, a sense of relief and freedom from all the terrible things I had been struggling with. I'm not saying I was fixed or that everything was alright now. I was still struggling at times, though not with the same intensity, but I could tell that God was beginning to break the chains and to cut the nets in which I had been trapped. In a mystery, it seemed that taking God's journey of forgiveness was beginning to bring me the relief and freedom I had been so desperately seeking for the past two years of my life, and the steppingstone of *blessing* was absolutely crucial on my journey. Praise be to God!

> *The ninth principle of forgiveness is this:*
> I need to not only forgive, but I also need to bless the one who hurt me so deeply.

Chapter #15

God's *journey of* forgiveness *was* *beginning to bring* me *the* relief *and* freedom *I had* *been so* desperately *seeking for.*

Sixteen
Releasing Them

Do not take revenge, my dear friends, but leave room
for God's wrath, for it is written: "It is mine to avenge;
I will repay," says the Lord.
Romans 12:19

The tenth steppingstone on the journey of forgiveness concerns *releasing* your offender to God. This means you let them
off your hook while trusting they're still on God's hook. Releasing them means accepting that you're not big enough,
smart enough, powerful enough, or wise enough to execute
justice in a proper way, so you release them to God, and you
let God be in charge of them and their sins, just like God is in
charge of you and your sins. Releasing them to God means
you're trusting that God knows exactly what they did to hurt
you so deeply, and that God sees your hurt and your pain and
your struggle and your trauma and that God isn't indifferent.
Releasing them means you're going to turn them over to God,
and you're going to let the Lord deal with them according to
his perfect heart and his perfect wisdom.

The following is a key passage that teaches the stepping-stone of releasing.

> *"Do not take revenge, my dear friends, but leave room*
> *for God's wrath, for it is written: 'It is mine to avenge; I*
> *will repay,' says the Lord."*
> (Romans 12:19)

It's interesting to note that in this verse God indicates not one time, but four times that we should trust him to take care of the person who has hurt us. It's as if God is saying, *"This particular point is so important that I'm going to say it one time in a certain way, but just in case you don't get the point, I'm going to go ahead and say it a second time in a little different way. But just in case you still don't get the point, I'm going to go ahead and say it a third way. And just in case you still haven't got the point, I'll go ahead and say it in a fourth way."*

I'd say this particular point must be pretty important for us to understand because it sure seems like God went above and beyond the call of duty to make it! Those four different ways of making the point that seems so important to God are:

1. Do not take revenge.
2. Leave room for God's wrath.
3. God will avenge.
4. God will repay.

In the metaphor of addition in a mathematical equation, we know that $2 + 2 + 2 + 2 = 8$. And in much the same way, it seems like something is "adding up" in this important scripture, and what's "adding up" is that God is more than able to handle your situation. God is not going to let your offender get away with anything. By the way, it's interesting to note that in point 3 just above, the meaning of the word "avenge" is *"to inflict harm upon one in return for an injury or wrong that's been done.*" Or, said another way, in God's Kingdom $2 + 2 + 2 + 2 = 8$, and you can trust that God is going to avenge the wrong that was done to you.

As I've been advancing on my journey of forgiveness, God placed it on my heart to listen to sermons and teachings on the topic of forgiveness, and I'm quite sure I've easily listened to at least fifty different messages. They've included teachings on forgiveness by Billy Graham, Chuck Swindoll, Charles Stanley, Tim Keller, John MacArthur, Corrie Ten Boom, David Wilkerson, Tony Evans, and Jentezen Franklin, among others.

While so many beautiful points were conveyed in many of these teachings, one particular idea that was shared in a sermon by Pastor Jimmy Evans deeply touched my heart. He told the story of a man that he truly resented during the early days of his ministry. This man didn't like Pastor Jimmy and did his very best to have him fired from the church. This provoked not only resentment in Pastor Jimmy's heart, but also ill will and even hatred. He was struggling deeply with dark thoughts and feelings toward this man. One day, as he was praying about the situation, he heard the Lord say to him, *"Jimmy, you see that man for what he's done to you, but I see him for what was done to him."* Pastor Jimmy said that God changed his heart in that moment, and he was relieved of his anger and resentment toward that man.

I think it's hard for us to forgive sometimes because we have an intuitive longing for justice. We know that what happened to us was so wrong, and we intuitively want it to be made right. This is why the cry of little kids' hearts is often, *"But that isn't fair!"* It's why we boo the bad guy in the movie and cheer for the good guy. We innately discern that certain things are deeply wrong in this very broken and unjust world, and our proclivity toward unforgiveness is a kind of kneejerk protest against the injustice we've suffered in our situation. We're afraid that if we forgive, it means the bad guys got away with what they did and that there's no justice in this world.

I don't think it's our longing for the injustice to be made right that's wrong in itself. In fact, I'd advocate that it's correct for us to long for justice and that this deep longing is actually a divine echo that lives deep in our hearts as image bearers of the very One who created us. So it's not the longing for justice that's wrong in itself, but it's often the "who" and the "when" that can be very misguided if we're not careful. *Who* gets to perpetrate the justice and *when* will the justice be perpetrated? And in our zeal, we often want to seize control of the process, and *I* want to perpetrate the justice *now*, according to my own preference and understanding. Releasing the one who has so deeply hurt us to God is, therefore, accepting the reality that we cannot see what God sees, we do not know what God knows, and we can trust God to judge and to avenge with his perfect wisdom, justice, and timing.

In view of what God was teaching me concerning "releasing," I wrote the following psalm entitled *Releasing Sheri & Her Divorce*, and I share a redacted version of the psalm here.

It's correct for us to long for justice, and this deep longing is actually a divine echo that lives deep in our hearts.

Psalm 514 – Releasing Sheri & Her Divorce

Dear God,

Good morning, Lord.

I thank you that you've given me another day of life.

I thank you for the birds I can hear singing this morning as the day is breaking.

They sing because you have given them voice, oh God, and they evidence the reality you intend, that there is song and joy and music and melody even in this very broken world.

I'm very grateful, God, that you're showing me a way forwad through the hurt and pain and darkness and torment and trauma I've been trapped in since Sheri left me on July 6, 2021, which was six-hundred and twenty-five days ago.

I've been seeking you, Lord, and beseeching you and pleading-with you to please deliver me from the power Sheri and her divorce have held over my heart and life and to break the invisible chains that have been holding me and to cut the invisible nets in which I've been entangled.

And while I was writing Psalm 513, Lord, Blessings over Sheri, you showed me the next step of my journey when you showed me I should next write a psalm of *releasing* Sheri.

So, this is my psalm to release Sheri and her divorce, after I have both forgiven her and blessed her.

And I pray, oh God, that as I release Sheri and her divorce to you, that you will release me from Sheri and her divorce.

I lay her and her divorce at your feet, oh God.

I have labored under the yoke of Sheri and the yoke of her divorce for the past six-hundred and twenty-five days, Lord, and it has been a burden that I cannot bear.

I pray, oh God, that you will take this burden as I release it to you, and I pray you take it off me and upon yourself, oh God.

I was never intended to carry this burden, Lord, because it is far too heavy for me.

I'm so thankful, Lord, that your shoulders are so much greater than mine and that you are so much stronger than me.

I thank you, oh God, that you care for me and that you want to take these burdens from my life.

I've tried to manage something that I'm completely incapable of managing, Lord, and I'm so grateful that you're willing to be my helper, Lord, if I will only allow myself to be helped by you.

By releasing Sheri and her divorce to you, Lord, I'm allowing you to assume complete authority and responsibility of both.

So I give both Sheri and her divorce to you, Lord, and I surrender them to you, and I turn them over to you for your safekeeping, and I release them to you.

I understand that I am not to take any form of vengeance, Lord, against any enemy or any person who has hurt or harmed or violated my life in any way.

I understand that vengeance belongs to you, Lord, and to you alone.

> *"Do not take revenge, my dear friends, but leave room*
> *for God's wrath, for it is written: 'It is mine to avenge; I*
> *will repay,' says the Lord."*
> (Romans 12:19)

I believe this, dear God, deeper in my heart at this moment than I have ever believed it.

I believe it so much, Lord, that it completely relieves me of any angst whatsoever about how or when or where you might choose to administer your perfect vengeance, oh God.

You have promised that you will avenge, oh God, and you will repay, and I know that I can trust you to do so, Lord.

I, therefore, say and announce that I release and relinquish any need for revenge whatsoever for any person or any situation.

I pray, oh God, that you will empower me by your Holy Spirit to remain in the place of humble trust in you to administer any judgment, vengeance, or wrath on my behalf, oh God.

By faith, I receive this day and this moment both relief and release from the burden I've quite mistakenly been carrying because of these things.

These things belong to you, oh God, and they do not belong to me, and I, therefore, release them to you, Lord, and I release them into your Kingdom.

In Jesus' Name and by the authority of Christ, I speak release, release, release, release, release, release, release, release, and release to you, oh God.

Thank you for hearing my prayer, Lord.

Thank you for your willingness to take from me that which I release to you.

Thank you, Jesus, that your yoke is easy, and your burden is light.

I'm so thankful that I can release my burdens to you, Lord, and in so doing, I am released from my burdens.

To God be the glory both now and forevermore.

In Jesus' Name I pray.

Amen.

The Tenth principle of forgiveness is this:
I need to release to God the one who has hurt me, trusting that He will deal with them according to his perfect heart and wisdom.

Seventeen
A Praise to God

As they began to sing and praise, the Lord set ambushes
against the men of Ammon and Moab and Mount Seir
who were invading Judah, and they were defeated.
II Chronicles 20:22

As I was working on the tenth steppingstone on the journey of forgiveness, which was "releasing" Sheri and her divorce to God, the Lord showed me what the eleventh steppingstone was going to be, and I felt he was asking me to write a psalm of *praise* to him. At first, I was a little confused, and I wondered what praise had to do with forgiveness. But as I considered the matter, I rather quickly could think of at least three situations in the bible where God gave the victory to his people in battle through the power of praise. In this way, praise actually becomes a weapon in the realm of the Kingdom. I knew I had been in one of the greatest battles of my life for the past two years, if not the single greatest battle, and if, in the inside out, upside down, backwards, and paradoxical Kingdom of God, he gives the victory to his people through the power of praise, then I was going to give God my praise.

The first example of the power of praise in battle is taken

from II Chronicles 20 when Jehoshaphat was King of Judah. As the story unfolds, Jehoshaphat is told that a vast army consisting of three different Kings is coming against Judah to destroy them. Jehoshaphat immediately turns to God for help and calls all of Judah to fasting and prayer. The next day, as they were going into battle, Jehoshaphat employs a very odd battle strategy as he sends the singers, singing praises to God, ahead of the army into the battle.

> *"After consulting the people, Jehoshaphat appointed men to sing to the Lord and to praise him for the splendor of his holiness as they went out at the head of the army, saying: 'Give thanks to the Lord, for his love endures forever.' As they began to sing and praise, the Lord set ambushes against the men of Ammon and Moab and Mount Seir who were invading Judah, and they were defeated."*
> (II Chronicles 20:21-22)

As the people sang praises to God, the Lord "set ambushes" against their enemies, and caused the bad guys to totally destroy themselves.

The second example of God giving victory to his people through shouts and praise is taken from the battle of Jericho. Again, we see that God gave his people a very odd battle plan when he told them to march around the city one time each day for six days, and to then march around the city seven times on the seventh day. The priests were then told to blow a long blast on their trumpets, and the army was told to give a loud shout and promised that the walls of Jericho would collapse.

> *"When the trumpets sounded, the army shouted, and at the sound of the trumpet, when the men gave a loud shout, the wall collapsed; so, everyone charged straight in, and they took the city."*
> (Joshua 6:21)

We see again that God caused the walls of Jericho to fall down through the odd obedience of the verbal proclamation of his people.

And the third example of God using the power of praise to give his people victory in battle is taken from the story of Gideon's army in Judges chapter 7. In this amazing story, God whittles Gideon's army from thirty-two thousand men down to only three-hundred men to fight a battle against one-hundred and thirty-five thousand Midianites. In the natural realm, that's totally crazy, and it's certainly a very counterintuitive battle strategy because it represented only one Israelite soldier to fight against every 450 Midianite soldiers. Again, God gives his people a very odd battle strategy when he tells them to go into the battle with four very unusual weapons, which were trumpets, clay pots, torches, and their voices. As the story unfolds, at the appointed time, Gideon had his men blow their trumpets, break their clay pots, hold up their torches, and shout with a loud shout, and when this happened, God threw the Midianite army into total chaos, and they turned upon themselves to completely destroy one another. Praise be to God!

When I understood the power of praise in battle, I wrote the following psalm of praise to God, and I share a redacted version of the psalm here.

If, in the inside out, upside down, backwards, and paradoxical kingdom of God, he gives the victory to his people through the power of praise, then I was going to give God my praise.

Psalm 515 – Praise and Glory to God

Dear God,

Good morning, Lord.

I begin this day by giving you praise, Lord, for you are worthy of praise.

You are the Almighty God.

You are the True and Living God.

You are the Supreme and Holy God.

You are high and lifted up.

You made the entire universe, including every planet and every star and every black hole and every quasar and every galaxy.

The universe is unimaginable in both its scope and mystery and indicates how great and magnificent you are, oh God, for the creator is greater than that which is created.

The Sistine Chapel came from the heart, mind, and hand of Michael Angelo, indicating what a brilliant artist he was, and the universe came from your heart, mind, and hand, indicating your incomprehensible magnificence and almighty power.

There is no one like you, Lord.

And you did this, oh God, by the supreme authority and power of your spoken word.

How can this be, Lord?

Who must you be, to have such magnificent and supreme power?

And within the economy of the human heart, Lord, supreme power often leads to supreme corruption, exploitation, and abuse, but within your heart and personhood, oh God, your supreme power and your supreme goodness dwell in perfect harmony.

Perfect power and supreme goodness together, alive, and powerful in one heart, in one person, and in one God.

I give you praise this day, oh God, for you are worthy of my praise.

And if you're both able and capable of running the entire universe, Lord, you must be capable of running my life, oh God.

For who am I and what am I, Lord?

I am incomprehensibly tiny and insignificant in the scope of the universe and in the scope of both time and eternity.

I am smaller than a speck.

The scope of my life is less than the blink of an eye in the ocean of the universe and the cosmic sea of eternity.

Yet you see me, Lord.

You care for me.

You know me.

You have made me your own, and I belong to you.

You condescend to, very patiently, wait for me and to whisper to me and to walk with me, even with my terrible proclivity to be suspicious of you and to doubt you and to be angry with you and to not trust you, as well as my terrible proclivity toward autonomy and pride and independence and mutiny and disobedience to you.

If you're really there, Lord, and I know you are, and if these things about you are really true, you truly are a great and amazing and mysterious and incomprehensible and surprising and almighty God.

Your creativity and imagination are on display everywhere, Lord.

The "data" that proves your existence is everywhere.

The beauty of your creation is stunning and breathtaking.

I read an article yesterday about the largest black hole they've ever identified in the universe, and this black hole is estimated to be forty billion times the mass of our sun, and it's emitting a quasar which is one-hundred and forty trillion times brighter than our sun.

This is simply incomprehensible, Lord.

And this is only *one* particular feature of the known universe.

How can this even be true, Lord?

And on the other end of the spectrum of your brilliant imagination and creativity, there are hummingbirds, which weigh an average of three grams each, which is about the weight of a penny.

And you know, Lord, that I don't even know what to say next.

The juxtaposition of these two magnificent expressions of your creative power and genius is simply incomprehensible and stunning.

Black holes and hummingbirds!

You are so amazing, Lord.

You are so magnificent.

You are so powerful.

You are so brilliant.

You are so creative.

You are so beautiful.

You are so mysterious.

The depths of who you are, Lord, can never be known, and yet you know me, and you invite me to know you.

You stand completely alone in your incomparable personhood and being.

There is no one like you, oh God.

You are so wonderful.

You are so glorious.

You are so radiant.

You are so good.

I struggle, oh God, to even find words in my feeble attempt to ascribe to you the wonder and glory and magnificence of who you are.

I give you my praise, oh God.

I acknowledge you, oh God.

And I know that I have not even begun to see or understand or comprehend the mysteries of who you must be, oh God.

My understanding of who you are, Lord, is incomprehensibly tiny compared to who you really are.

I suspect that this is much of what eternity will be, Lord, as we who are your creation will forever plumb the depths and explore the wonders and mysteries and intricacies and richness of who you are.

We will be coming to know the God who can never be fully known.

No matter how long we dig and explore the depths of who you are, oh God, we will never come to the end of discovery, for there will forever be so much more of you to know.

For you, alone, are God.

You, alone, are the Almighty God.

You, alone, are the true and living God.

You, alone, are the One who is high and lifted up.

You, alone, are the most beautiful and magnificent God.

And you, alone, are worthy of all praise and honor and glory and worship forever and forever and forevermore.

Please forgive my horrible and unforgiveable proclivity to underestimate and diminish who you truly are, Lord.

If I could even begin to comprehend your greatness, I would surely collapse on the ground in utter and overwhelming awe of who you are.

If I could even see one tiny iota of your glory, I would surely be stunned, if not completely crushed by the weight of your glorious beauty and splendor.

I am so grateful, oh God, that I have you and that I'm beginning to know something of who you are.

I've spent my life devoted to you, Lord, and you are so worthy of my devotion.

I pray I will be forever captured and enraptured by your beauty and by your person and by your glory and by the supreme greatness of who you are.

This day I say from my heart, oh God, glory be to God, glory be to God, glory be to God, glory be to God.

Glory be to you, oh God, both now and forevermore.

In Jesus' Name I pray.

Amen.

> *The eleventh principle of forgiveness is this:*
> I need to offer God a sacrifice of praise as a spiritual weapon in the battle of forgiveness.

Eighteen

A Letter to Them

[23] "Therefore, if you are offering your gift at the altar and there remember that your brother or sister has something against you,[24] leave your gift there in front of the altar. First go and be reconciled to them; then come and offer your gift.
Matthew 5:34-24

Please note an important distinction between this twelfth steppingstone and steppingstone seven, which was *"Forgiving Them."* In steppingstone seven, I wrote a psalm in which I was talking to God about my forgiveness of Sheri. By contrast, in this steppingstone, I felt led by the Lord to actually write a letter of forgiveness to Sheri herself. When God showed me to do this, I realized it was important because I shouldn't just tell God that I'm forgiving Sheri, but I should also tell Sheri that I'm forgiving Sheri. Of course, I don't know that I'll ever give the letter I wrote to Sheri because, at this point, I'm not sure she'd have any interest in hearing words of "forgiveness" from me, and I don't think she even thinks she's done anything wrong against me. I might be wrong, but I suspect she'd do nothing more than scoff at the suggestion that she even needs to be forgiven by me. My suspicion is that this dynamic is quite common because the person being forgiven quite often would disagree with what the person doing the forgiving is even forgiving them for in the first place.

For example, in my situation, I might say, *"Sheri, I forgive you for giving up on me, and for giving up on us, and for giving up on the Lord."* And I feel this is true because I think Sheri gave up on all three, and in so doing, she absolutely broke my heart. But Sheri might completely disagree with my assessment that she gave up on me and on us and on the Lord, and she, no doubt, has a line of reasoning established within herself that explains why she had to do what she chose to do and why she's completely justified in her action. So what do you do when the person you're forgiving doesn't even agree with what you're forgiving them for?

I'd advocate the right answer is that you just go ahead and forgive them anyway. Because you live in your skin, and you see the world through your eyes, and you experienced the situation the way you experienced it, and your offense is your offense, and your hurt is your hurt. So you need to forgive them for what you need to forgive them for, whether they agree with what you're forgiving them for or not. The reality is that I was writing my letter of forgiveness to Sheri to process the violations of relationship and the sins she perpetrated against me that were both felt and real to *me*, and I was writing in obedience toward the hope that God would set me free from the chains and nets in which I had been entangled.

It's interesting to observe that in the parable of the unforgiving servant that Jesus shared in Matthew 18, the servant was forgiven by his master a debt of ten thousand bags of gold that he could have never repaid. You'd think that experiencing such an extravagant expression of forgiveness would have deeply and profoundly affected him and gone a long way toward the softening of his own heart, but that's not at all what happened. Instead, he turned around and "seized" a fellow servant that owed him only one hundred pieces of silver, and he refused to forgive his fellow servant. In fact, not only did he not forgive his fellow servant, but he also had him thrown into prison until he could repay the debt, which is absurd because how in the world would the guy ever be able to repay the debt if he was stuck in prison?

This part of the story reveals a very important principle of forgiveness, which is that the forgiveness you offer another person may not even be recognized or appreciated by them, and it may not have any affect in changing them or changing their heart in any way. The servant had been forgiven a significant debt by his master, but his heart apparently remained cold, hard, unbroken, unrepentant, and unchanged. How sad.

Regardless of Sheri's response, I knew the right thing for me to do was to forgive her and that God wanted me to forgive her, and I needed to forgive her. I needed to forgive Sheri for me, if not for her. I was sincerely interested in doing the work God was calling me to do, and he had shown me that this would be the twelfth steppingstone on my journey of forgiveness. I needed to write a letter to Sheri expressing my forgiveness to her, so I wrote the following psalm in order to do so. Please note that this is a redacted version of the psalm, and in the body of the psalm itself, I specifically named "seventy-eight" different things for which I was forgiving Sheri that I am not disclosing here.

You need to forgive them for what you need to forgive them for, whether they agree with what you're forgiving them for or not.

Psalm 527 – Forgiving Sheri

Dear Sheri,

I'm writing this letter to you to forgive you for the many ways you've so deeply hurt my heart and my life.

I'm writing this letter to forgive you for all the pain and trauma you've caused me.

I know that I was not a perfect husband, just as you were not a perfect wife, but I loved you and I adored you with all my heart.

I was completely devoted to you, to our marriage, to our wedding vows, to our family, and to our future, and I took care of you for over 40 years.

I do not believe I deserved what you did to me for at least three very important reasons.

Because I cannot see that you had any biblical grounds whatsoever for your divorce, and you never offered me any explanation that would even begin to approximate biblical grounds for your divorce.

Because I appealed to you over, and over, and over again to tell me what you needed from me in order to remain in the fight for our marriage, and I would have done *absolutely anything* that you asked of me or needed from me, and you refused to even communicate with me in any meaningful way whatsoever.

And because we are believers in Christ, and we are God followers, and we belonged to God, and we always served God, and God is a God of hope, and power, and healing, and redemption, and resurrection, and life, and God would have helped us, and God would have made a way for us, because God was for us, and he was not against us.

The Lord says that I need to forgive you Sheri, so I do forgive you.

He says that I myself will be forgiven in the way that I forgive others, so I forgive you.

He says that I should forgive you the 100 silver coins that you owe me, because I myself have been forgiven a debt of 10,000 bags of gold, so I forgive you.

I forgive you Sheri, for...

I forgive you Sheri, for...

I forgive you Sheri, for...

I forgive you Sheri, for...

(Enumeration of at least seventy-eight things I'm forgiving Sheri for here.)

I forgive you, Sheri, for all these things, and for anything and everything else you've done to hurt me and to violate my personhood and to harm me and to sin against me and to cause me to have the greatest hurt and pain and trauma of my life.

You ripped my soul out, and you caused my heart to bleed, and bleed, and bleed, but I forgive you.

I forgive you, Sheri.

I forgive you, Sheri.

I forgive you, Sheri.

I forgive you, and I bless you, and I release both you and your divorce to God in Jesus' Name.

I speak this forgiveness over you in faith and obedience to God.

I speak this forgiveness over you as one who, myself, is in desperate need of forgiveness and one who has been forgiven by the Great Forgiver.

From the man who was your husband for 39 years, 10 months, and 3 days.

Tony

The Lord says that
I need to forgive
you Sheri, so I
do forgive you.

Nineteen
The Holy Fire

¹⁹ A number who had practiced sorcery brought their scrolls together and burned them publicly. When they calculated the value of the scrolls, the total came to fifty thousand drachmas. ²⁰ In this way the word of the Lord spread widely and grew in power.
Acts 19:19-20

It's interesting to note that in the bible God uses fire over and over again in unusual ways toward his Kingdom purposes.

- God called Moses through a burning bush. (Exodus 3:2-3)

- God led his people through the wilderness with a pillar of cloud by day and a pillar of fire by night. (Exodus 13:21-22)

- In the Old Testament, the entire Hebrew sacrificial system was based upon God's people making burnt offerings to the Lord through the fires of sacrifice. (Leviticus 17)

- When the prophet Elijah faced 850 prophets of Baal on Mount Carmel, God consumed Elijah's sacrifice with fire from heaven, even after Elijah had doused the altar with twelve barrels of water. (I Kings 18:38-39)

- God protected the three Hebrew boys, Shadrach, Meshach, and Abednego from the fiery furnace when they refused to bow down in worship of King Nebuchadnezzar's golden statue. (Daniel 3:24-25)

- As a manifestation of the Holy Spirit, tongues of fire appeared upon each of the disciples on the day of Pentecost. (Acts 2:1-4)

There's another example of fire being used in an unusual way when the apostle Paul was in the city of Ephesus. Paul was there preaching the gospel, and as a result, some sorcerers came to faith in Christ (Acts 19:17-20). Because of their new-found faith, they presumably realized they could no longer practice their occultic sorceries, so they brought together the various paraphernalia they had been using for such practices (maybe scrolls, writings, potions, skulls, crystals, astrological charts, etc.) and in an act of obedience, to cleanse themselves of their old way of life, they burned all these things publicly. They had what I call a *Holy Fire*, or maybe better said, a *Holy Bonfire* because the passage indicates the pile of artifacts was so large it was innumerable, and the cumulative value of everything that was burned was an enormous amount of money.

Based upon this passage in Acts 19, I've used literal fire as a spiritual intervention in my own life, and as a Licensed Professional Counselor, I've also used the Holy Fire as an intervention in the lives of others. For example, I might suggest to a client that they write a letter to their mother who passed away seventeen years before: *"If you could talk to your mother one more time for an hour, what would you need to say to her now that you were unable to say to her seventeen years ago?"*

The client writes the letter, we do some therapeutic work around the letter, and then we make a literal fire in the fire pit, and the client offers the letter as a burnt sacrifice to the Lord through the flames of the Holy Fire. In so doing, I'm attempting to help the person face and process some unsettled business that's typically way overdue and then give them the opportunity to release those things to the Lord as they receive his grace and healing in their heart and life. I believe that when a person offers such a sacrifice to the Lord from a sincere heart, that as the smoke and aroma of that sacrifice smolders its way into heaven and into the nostrils of God, it's a sacrifice that's well pleasing to him, just as the burnt offerings of his people in the Old Testament were pleasing to him. The Holy Fire is a therapeutic intervention that provides catharsis and closure in many situations.

Over the years, I've hosted many Holy Fires for groups of men as part of the Power of Purity ministry. I invite the men to bring a "sacrifice" to offer to God through the flames of the Holy Fire, including anything they feel convicted to cleanse out of their life, in the same way the sorcerers were cleansing their lives of their magical arts in Acts 19. I've witnessed men sacrifice computers, iPads, cell phones, porn magazines, porn movies, XXX books, little black books with the names and phone numbers of prostitutes, photos and letters from past mistresses, and copies of their sexual inventory, among many other such items. It's always a very powerful and moving experience to participate in a Holy Fire, and it's typically a strategic steppingstone on the healing journey for many men.

And that's the very reason I believe God was leading me to have a Holy Fire as the thirteenth and final steppingstone on my journey of forgiveness. In fact, as the final days of my marriage were unfolding, I ended up having two separate Holy Fire's. The first one was witnessed by the men at the weekly purity group I've attended for over the past twenty years,

I believe that when a person offers such a sacrifice to the Lord from a sincere heart, that as the smoke and aroma of that sacrifice smolders its way into heaven and into the nostrils of God, it's well pleasing to him, just as the burnt offerings of his people in the Old Testament were pleasing to him.

and the second one was witnessed by my dear sister, Candy, and my dear brother-in-law, Brian. If possible, I always prefer to have witnesses at a Holy Fire because it seems a significant principle of God's Kingdom is that spiritual things are established in the company of witnesses. Toward my purpose here I'll share just a bit about the second of these Holy Fire's.

For many years I had a small picture of Sheri and I from our wedding that was very meaningful to me. In this picture we had turned around from the altar and we were walking back down the aisle after just being pronounced husband and wife. We had not even been married for one minute, and under our picture was the beautiful promise:

"For I know the plans I have for you," declares the Lord, "plans to prosper you and not to harm you, plans to give you a future and a hope." (Jeremiah 29:11)

This picture was very important to me, and I looked at it frequently as it had been in my home office for many years. When Sheri therefore left me on July 6th, 2021, and then subsequently filed for divorce, the picture became a stabbing heartache to me every time I looked at it. With all my heart I did not believe my wife's divorce was the heart, mind, or will of God for our lives, and I therefore placed the picture directly under another picture that held great meaning to me. This other picture is that of Jesus with the crown of thorns on his head with his head bowed in obedient submission to the Father. I therefore placed our wedding picture directly under the picture of Jesus, and in this way, I was trusting that Jesus was looking down upon our marriage, upon our wedding vows, and upon our very difficult situation. I left the wedding picture there for the next two years as I appealed to my wife over and over, and as I prayed to God to intervene in our situation and to rescue our marriage.

As the situation therefore advanced toward the completion of my wife's divorce, I eventually was forced to leave our marital home, which I had lived in and loved for over twenty years, and after slowly packing and moving over a period of months, one of the very last things that remained in the house was these two pictures of Jesus watching over our marriage. As I contemplated what to do with these pictures, and particularly with the picture from the very first minute of our marriage, I simply didn't know what to do with them, and one day I had a conversation with my friend CJ about this matter.

"I don't know what to do with this picture CJ. I don't think I really want to take it with me because it hurts so much every time I look at it. But I don't feel right about just throwing it in the trash, so I just don't know what to do."

"Why don't you have a Holy Fire Tony, and give that picture to the Lord?"

As soon as CJ said those words, they resonated deeply within my heart, and I immediately knew that this is exactly what I needed to do with the picture. I therefore determined that the very last thing I would do before leaving the home we had lived in for over twenty years was to have a Holy Fire before the Lord. I invited my sister and my brother-in-law to be witnesses, and on my very last evening at the house, as the very last thing I would ever do at that house, I gave God a number of different gifts through the consuming flames of the Holy Fire. These gifts included:

- Several of my mother's bible study pages that were written by my mother's own hand. These pages were very meaningful to me, and I had posted them on the kitchen cabinets as a source of encouragement as I struggled through the previous two years.

- Another page containing a quote from a book entitled "Finding Meaning" by author David Kessler, where he speaks of the important difference between being alive and actually living, and the importance of choosing to *live* after a great loss in your life.

- The several pages of a prayer altar I had posted on the wall on behalf of my sons, asking God to break any familiar spirits and generational curses that remained upon our family.

- Two different psalms I had written to the Lord, including psalm 601 entitled, *My Last Day at El Caballo*, and psalm 602 entitled, *A Final Prayer*, which was a final prayer I had written to God on behalf of our marriage while Sheri and I were still husband and wife, and a copy of which I had sent to my wife.

- And most importantly, the picture of Sheri and I that had been taken over 39 years earlier from the first minute of our marriage.

The picture was the very last thing I placed in the fire, and it was the hardest thing of all to surrender to the Lord. I struggled deeply to let go of that picture, and as I held it in my hands for the very last time, looking at the young couple who was filled with such joy and hope, my heart was completely broken all over again and I may have cried the deepest tears I've ever cried from the very depths of my soul. After several extended moments of deep grief, I finally kissed the picture, and I placed it in the flames of the Holy Fire, not because I wanted to, but because I knew I had to.

I watched as the flames consumed the sacrifices I was giving to God. The smoke and the aroma smoldered its way into heaven, and I trusted that my sacrifices were pleasing to the Lord. I cried, and I prayed, and both my sister and my brother-in law said prayers over me and over the gifts that were smoldering in the fire. It was the very last thing I did at 2 El Caballo, the home we had lived in for over twenty years, and in retrospect I think it was the most appropriate thing I could have ever done, as that Holy Fire represented a bridge of faith I was crossing from my past into my unknown future, both of which God was holding in his hands.

I was crossing from my past into my unknown future, both of which God was holding in his hands.

Chapter 19.

The following is psalm 577 which I wrote to God in preparation of the first Holy Fire I had with my men's group.

Psalm 577– The Holy Fire

Dear Almighty God and Heavenly Father,

I'm writing this prayer for the Holy Fire that's taking place tomorrow evening.

I've been looking forward to the Holy Fire, and I'm excited to meet you there Lord.

As you know Lord, my wife left me on July 6th, 2021, and filed for divorce, and as a result the past two years have been the hardest two years of my entire life.

I do not believe my wife's divorce is your will for our lives Lord, but it's what my wife is choosing, and I've been absolutely powerless to do anything about it.

It's been the most painful and hurtful thing I've ever experienced in my entire life, and I've struggled, and struggled, and struggled, and struggled in so many ways.

I've prayed and prayed that you might intervene in our situation Lord, and I presented my divine lawsuit to you in defense of our marriage.

But so far Lord, nothing has changed that I can see.

I didn't think anything could ever hurt me more than my wife leaving me, but I was wrong, because I found out 12 weeks ago that my wife is with another man, and that twisted the knife that was already in my heart even deeper than ever before.

At times I've been so tormented Lord, and so upset, and so overwhelmed, and so beside myself.

I've wondered at times if I might be going crazy, and it's seemed like I would never be the same.

It's been like getting cut in half Lord, and I don't know how to get cut in half.

I've felt smothered and suffocated, and it's like I'm trapped in chains and entangled in nets.

I've been grieving Lord, deeper than I've ever grieved before, because this has been the single greatest loss of my entire life.

I need you to help me Lord, and I need you to do something for me that I can't do for myself.

And you've shown me that I need to forgive my wife Lord, and that by forgiving her I myself will be set free.

So I began my journey of forgiveness, and I'm trying to forgive her Lord, not just in my head, but in my heart.

But I don't think I'm a very good forgiver Lord, but I'm trying to figure it out.

So this night oh God, I bring all that I am to you, and I give all that I am to you through the flames of this Holy Fire.

I make a sacrifice of myself to you Lord.

I give my heart to you.

I give my life to you.

I give my marriage to you.

I give my wife to you.

I give our wedding vows to you.

I give my wife's divorce to you.

I give my future to you.

I give my hurt and my pain to you.

I give my grief to you.

I give my betrayal trauma to you.

I give my wife and her relationship with this man to you.

I give my ministry to you oh God.

I give my journey of forgiveness to you.

I give all my failures and weaknesses to you.

I give all my questions to you, and I give all my doubts to you.

I give you my anger, and my rage, and my upset, and my confusion, and my torment, and my bitterness, and my hatred, and my thoughts of revenge and vengeance.

And I give you this book that I've written about forgiveness.

And I give you all these psalms, and prayers, and laments, and rants that I've written.

I acknowledge my need for you oh God.

I acknowledge that I'm lost without you.

I acknowledge that I'm desperate for you Lord.

I pray oh God that you will receive these gifts and sacrifices that I offer to you this night through the flames of the Holy Fire.

I pray that these gifts and sacrifices might be pleasing to you oh God.

I pray that you will receive these gifts and sacrifices from my heart to your heart oh God.

I pray the aroma and fragrance of these gifts and sacrifices will be a pleasing aroma to you Lord.

I pray oh God, that as these gifts and sacrifices burn in this literal fire, and are consumed, that you will do something powerful and holy in my heart oh God, that only you can do.

I pray oh God that you will burn from me, and consume from me, any chains, or nets, or bondages, or encumbrances, or strongholds, or captivities, or lies, that hold any place within my heart, soul, or life.

I beseech thee oh God, with all my heart, to do something within me that I cannot do for myself.

I pray that you will fill me with the Holy Spirit and pray that you will fill me with your peace, and with your strength, and with your power.

I pray oh God that you will renounce from me any demon, or power, or principality, or spirit, that holds any place within me oh God.

I pray that you will rebuke the enemy from my life oh God, and I pray that you bring forth your Kingdom within me.

I say that you are the Almighty, and Wonderful, and All Powerful, and All Knowing, and Incomprehensible God.

I give myself to you Lord.

I cry out to you oh God.

I call upon you Lord, and I put my hope in you, and I say, blessed be the Name of the Lord both now and forevermore.

I pray these things in the Name of my Savior, Jesus, and I pray for the His powerful blood over both my life and over these gifts and sacrifices to you oh God.

In Jesus' Name I pray.

Amen.

The thirteenth principle of forgiveness is this:
I should consider having a Holy Fire where I offer to God a particular object or objects as a literal sacrifice representing the situation or person I'm seeking to forgive.

Recognize that forgiveness is an important tool that's absolutely non-negotiable for successful relationship.

Twenty

Honorable Mentions

So watch yourselves. "If your brother or sister
sins against you, rebuke them; and if they repent, forgive them.
Luke 17:3

You now know the thirteen steppingstones that God revealed to me on my journey of forgiveness. They are as follows:

1. God's way of forgiveness is counterintuitive.

2. I should seek to understand what God says about forgiveness.

3. Forgiveness is an exercise and obedience of your will regardless of your emotions.

4. Your ability to forgive will be directly related to your ability to grieve the hurt and pain you've suffered.

5. You can forgive others when you realize how much you yourself have been forgiven.

6. I should do a comprehensive inventory of my own sins and defects of character to realize how much I myself need forgiveness.

7. I need to articulate and proclaim to God my actual statement of forgiveness for the one who has hurt me.

8. I should understand that forgiveness is not an event, but a process, and I may need to forgive the person who has hurt me, over and over again.

9. I need to not only forgive, but I also need to bless the one who hurt me so deeply.

10. I need to release to God the one who has hurt me, trusting that He will deal with them according to his perfect heart and wisdom.

11. I need to offer God a sacrifice of praise as a spiritual weapon in the battle of forgiveness.

12. I should write a letter to articulate my forgiveness to the person I'm actually forgiving, which I may or may not actually share with them.

13. I should consider having a Holy Fire where I offer to God a particular object or objects as a literal sacrifice representing the situation or person I'm seeking to forgive.

I'd like to finalize my thoughts by sharing a few "honorable mentions" concerning forgiveness that are included for free! There are four of them specifically.

The first one is to recognize that forgiveness is an important tool that's absolutely non-negotiable for successful relationship. In fact, I'd advocate that you cannot have successful relationship if you don't have this tool in your relational toolbox. The reason for this is because, in the context of close relationships, there will *inevitably* be misunderstandings, differences of viewpoint and opinion, hurt feelings, disagreements, arguments, and other such relational difficulties. And what are we to do when we bump into these difficult situations? I'd advocate that this is why the tool of forgiveness is so critically important: it's forgiveness that creates the possibility for people to traverse difficult relational territory in both directions, from me to you and from you to me. If I realize I've done something to hurt or offend you, I can seek your forgiveness, and if you're hurt or offended me, I can seek to offer you forgiveness, and in this way, it becomes possible for us to transition the difficult episode as we move forward in our relationship. I'd suggest the longevity of any relationship will be seriously jeopardized if the people in that relationship are not able to access and utilize the tool of forgiveness in the context of their hearts and relationship. It's of absolute critical importance.

The second honorable mention is to recognize that forgiveness is not the same as reconciliation. I think part of what makes forgiveness seem so difficult sometimes is the misunderstanding that if I forgive someone for what they've done to me, that it means everything is now alright between the two of us, and nothing could be further from the truth. The fact is that forgiveness only takes one person, but reconciliation takes two people, and reconciliation is predicated upon the offender's repentance. If they refuse to acknowledge what they've done to hurt you, and they refuse to take responsibility for what they've done, and they refuse to say they're sorry or ask for forgiveness, then you're not expected to be reconciled to them in the relationship as if everything is now alright. You can forgive them for what they did to you, but that doesn't mean you have to be reconciled to them in the relationship. Imagine how torturous it would feel to be compelled into a relationship with a person who has deeply hurt you, while you're expected to just "suck it up" and pretend like everything's alright, while in the meantime, the offender hasn't even acknowledged or apologized in any way for the offense. No wonder so many people have such a struggle with forgiveness if this is what they think forgiveness is. In the story of the prodigal son in Luke 15, the father was watching the horizon for the return of his wayward son, but it wasn't until the son returned in humility and repentance that the father was then able to do what he always wanted to do, which was to bless his son with hugs, kisses, and parties.

The third honorable mention is the single most important thing that can ever be said about forgiveness. You'll remember the main point that Jesus conveyed in the parable of the unforgiving servant in Matthew 18 is that we should forgive others based upon the reality that we, ourselves, have been forgiven. It's, therefore, of utmost importance that we each receive the forgiveness the Master offers us in exchange for the debt we could never repay, or said another way, we must each receive the forgiveness of our sins from the Great Forgiver, himself, and it's his kind and undeserved forgiveness toward us that will then enable us to become the forgivers he's calling us to be. God loves us, and he proved his great love by sending his only begotten son, Jesus Christ, to die on the cross for our sins so we might be saved. Jesus then rose from the dead three days later to prove that he is the son of the living God, and he offers the wonderful gift of forgiveness to all who will believe in him and receive him as their Savior.

> *13 For he has rescued us from the dominion of darkness and brought us into the kingdom of the Son he loves, 14 in whom we have redemption, the forgiveness of sins.*
> (Colossians 1:13-14)

If you've never done so before, I invite you, dear friend, to open your heart and to receive Jesus as your personal Savior so your sins might be forgiven and that you might become a child of God.

And the fourth and final honorable mention, with which I'll conclude this book, is a metaphor the Lord gave me when I began writing the book. Imagine if you put all kinds of things in the gas tank of your car that weren't supposed to go in the gas tank. What if you put some milk in your gas tank, some paint, some shampoo, some water, turpentine, and some liquid plumber? Obviously, all these things would be terribly inconsistent with how your car was designed to run, and they would, no doubt, dramatically affect your car's ability to function properly. In much the same way, when we allow unforgiveness to live in our heart and life, it puts all these toxic ingredients within our soul that are very counterproductive to the way God designed us to function as healthy human beings. It's like putting hatred, bitterness, resentment, rage, and vengeance in the metaphorical "gas tank" of a human being's heart, all of which are very toxic and counterproductive to their health and prosperity. This, my friend, is why we need to forgive, because it's in forgiving them that *we* are set free.

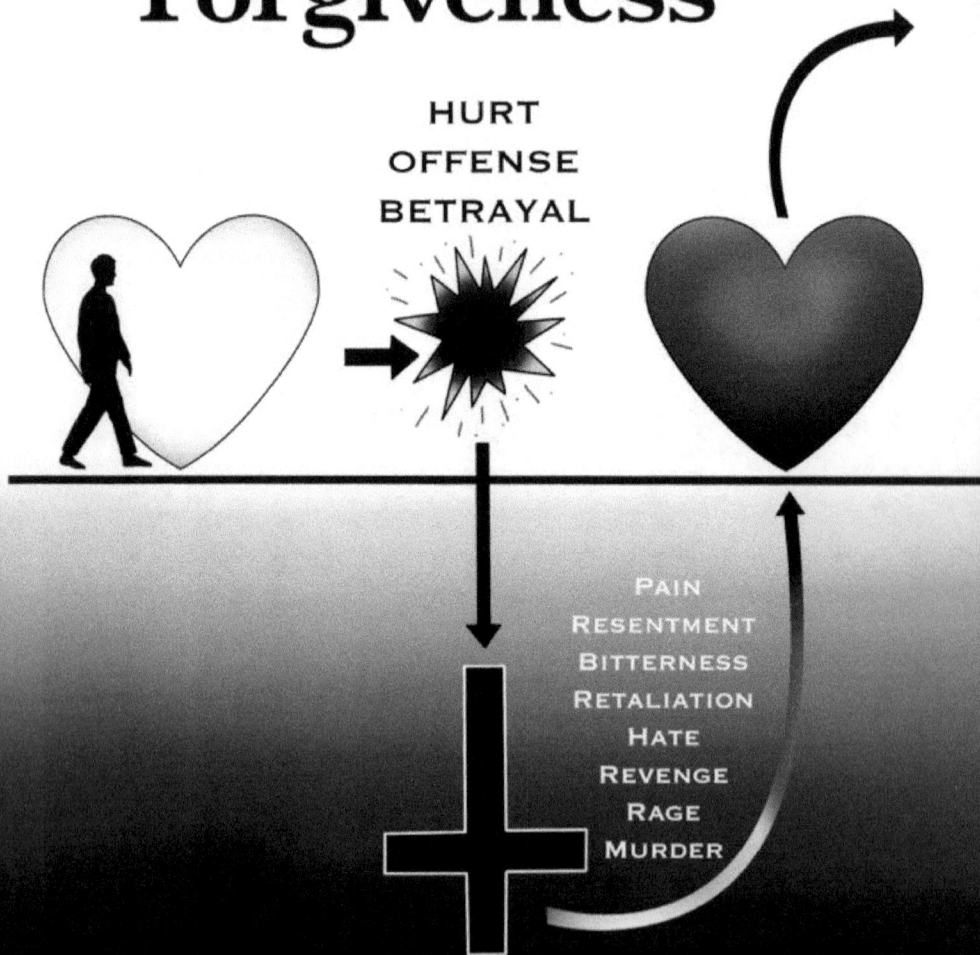

KINGDOM

The Journey of Forgiveness

HURT
OFFENSE
BETRAYAL

PAIN
RESENTMENT
BITTERNESS
RETALIATION
HATE
REVENGE
RAGE
MURDER

KINGDOM OF

OF LIGHT

1. Accept the counterintuitive pathway of God
2. Reflect upon key forgiveness passages
3. Will to forgive despite your emotions
4. Grieve your pain and loss
5. Realize you can forgive because you've been forgiven
6. Reflect upon what you've been forgiven of
7. Forgive them for what they've done
8. Embrace the repetitive work of forgiveness
9. Bless them
10. Release them to God
11. Give praise to God
12. Write a letter of forgiveness to them
13. Offer God a gift through the Holy Fire

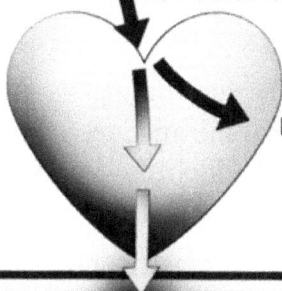

REST
PEACE
RELIEF
FREEDOM

PAIN
RESENTMENT
BITTERNESS
RETALIATION
HATE
REVENGE
RAGE
MURDER

DARKNESS

Addendum 1

Observations from Forgiveness Diagram

1. The path the person is walking on represents the forward progress of their life through time.

2. There's a spiritual battle raging around this person, which is illustrated by the kingdom of light above them and the kingdom of darkness below them.

3. At some point on their journey, another person deeply hurts, offends or betrays them, which is represented by the black starburst.

4. When this deep hurt occurs, their heart becomes filled with poisons such as: pain, resentment, bitterness, retaliation, hate, revenge, rage, and murder.

5. It's not necessarily that these poisons are placed in the person's heart from the outside, as much as the hurtful situation exposes and cultivates what already lives in the person's own sinful heart.

6. The person is now in a place of darkness, bondage, and captivity as represented by the darkness that now lives in their heart. The green beast is on them.

7. At some point, the person realizes they cannot go on living this way, so they turn to Jesus to take the journey of forgiveness.

8. The journey of forgiveness is not necessarily an easy journey, and it will require both time and effort, but the person realizes they must take this journey.

9. The person is now walking their journey of forgiveness, which includes the 13 steppingstones of forgiveness as reflected in this book:

1. God's Pathway is Counterintuitive

2. Key Bible Passages on Forgiveness

3. Will Over Emotions

4. Grief

5. The Power Principle of Forgiveness

6. Forgive Me My Debts

7. Forgiving Them

8. The Work of Forgiveness

9. Blessing Them

10. Releasing Them

11. A Praise to God

12. A Letter to Them

13. The Holy Fire

10. As the person continues forward on their journey of forgiveness and does the corresponding work of forgiveness, the power of forgiveness permeates and saturates deeper and deeper into their heart and pushes the poisons of unforgiveness out of their heart, back to the pits of hell where they belong.

11. The person now experiences genuine rest, peace, relief, and freedom because true freedom comes through forgiveness.

Addendum 2

The Three Tenses of Forgiveness

In much the same way there are three tenses of time (the past, the present, the future), and there are three tenses of salvation (justification, sanctification, glorification), I've come to believe through my "journey of forgiveness" that there are also three tenses of forgiveness: I have not forgiven, I'm forgiving, and I have forgiven. Let me try to explain.

As the time I'm writing this addendum entitled *The Three Tenses of Forgiveness*, I've been working on this book for almost two years, and you might think that since I've now written a book of the topic of forgiveness, that I'd be an "expert forgiver" by now. But nothing could be further from the truth, and at the very best I'd advocate that I might be in forgiveness first grade, or maybe second grade. Or, said another way, as I've continued to move forward on my journey of forgiveness, seeking to apply to my life the thirteen principles of forgiveness that I've shared in this book, I've also continued to struggle with the practical application of forgiveness in my personal situation. At times I've genuinely felt forgiveness toward the person who hurt my heart and my life so deeply (I have forgiven), at other times I've struggled deeply as I've tried to align my personal experience with the theology I profess to believe about forgiveness (I am forgiving), and at other times I've felt the hurt, pain, and angst over what happened so acutely that it made me feel like I was all the way back at square one and had to start the process all over again (I have not forgiven). And then, as if this wasn't already confusing enough to feel these various and conflicting feelings about forgiveness in my head and heart, much of the time I was feeling all three of these aspects of forgiveness, all at the same time! This made we wonder if I might actually be crazy, because how in the world could I be feeling like I'm forgiving someone, and trying to forgive them, and feeling like I can't forgive, all at the same time? And this is when I realized that there are actually three tenses of forgiveness (I have not forgiven, I'm forgiving, and I have forgiven), that a person can experience all three of these tenses at the same time, and that doing so doesn't mean you're crazy, and only means you're human.

Addendum 3

Why Did Tony Write This Book?

Although there are many thoughts I could share concerning why I've written this book, I'll share just two of the primary reasons here.

I published my first book, *Stories*, over 20 years ago, and in that book, I shared much of the story and the brokenness of my life. Talking about my own life, pain, failures, struggles, and my own pathway of redemption has been the centerpiece of my life and my ministry ever since then and has had many expressions over the years including my books, my counseling, my prison ministry, my men's groups, my intensives, and my podcast. It's what I do and it's who I am. And further, I believe it's literally my calling in the Kingdom of God, it's how I serve the Lord, and it's how God has used my life and my voice to encourage and help countless others. In a mystery, I've learned that what helps others the most is when I honestly and transparently share my own failures, struggles, pain, and how God is working in my life as a result. And in view of this I'm now sharing about the experience of the divorce because I consider it the single biggest loss of my life, and the single biggest failure of my life, and the single biggest trauma of my life, and because of this I cannot not share about it.

But that's still not the main reason I wrote the book.

When my ex-wife left me and filed for divorce, it catapulted me into the most painful and darkest days of my entire life, and into an existential crisis that made me struggle deeply with the question of my very existence. As I limped and groped my way forward on my difficult journey, I was eventually deeply affected by the cumulative voices and work of several key people, most notably Jordan Peterson (*We Who Wrestle with God*), Victor Frankl (*Mans Search for Meaning*), David Kessler (*Finding Meaning*), and Bessel Van Der Kolk (*The Body Keeps the Score*). As I read and researched what these amazing teachers were sharing, a very important theme began to emerge that informed me in a significant way.

The essence of that theme was that the antidote to the inevitable pain we experience in this life is ultimately found in *meaning*. Or said another way, the way to endure the pain you're suffering is to find a higher and transcendent *meaning* that becomes greater than the pain itself. This revelation was of profound significance to me because I was essentially drowning and suffocating in the deepest pain and greatest torment of my entire life, and it was in this dark and desperate place that God (I believe) eventually showed me that the only way out of my own pain and torment was through the unexpected, counterintuitive, and odd pathway of forgiveness. I was going to have to forgive the person who had hurt me more than anyone has ever hurt me in my entire life, and that became a significant crisis for me because *I could not do it*. And when I say I couldn't do it, the best way I can explain what I mean is with the following example. Imagine that for some reason you were super angry one day. Maybe even more angry than you've ever been before, even to the point of seething rage. But then, at that very moment, in the midst of this intense anger and rage, you try to make it all go away by saying the words out loud to yourself, *"I'm not angry! I'm not angry! I'm not angry!"* Your words would in fact feel impotent against the enormity of the raging emotion that you're actually feeling on the inside of you. In much the same way, I kept trying to say to myself, *"I forgive Sheri! I forgive Sheri! I forgive Sheri!"*. But I knew that my words were a complete hypocrisy when compared with the reality of what really lived in my heart at the time. I was saying *"I forgive Sheri"* on the outside of me, but I knew that I was nowhere near genuine forgiveness on the inside of me, and I had no idea of how to reconcile the dramatic disparity between these two conflicting realities. As a Christian I believed in forgiveness in my head and theology, but when it came to the practical reality of my real-life situation, it seemed impossible for me to truly forgive the person who had hurt me so deeply. And thus began my "journey of forgiveness". I told God that I would try to forgive if he would show me how, and if he would help me, and that's exactly what happened as my "journey of forgiveness" began to slowly unfold as revealed through the story of this book.

And it was only then, through the difficult but redemptive process that God had called me to, that I began to slowly discover a higher purpose and *meaning* in my suffering. Maybe my pain and what I was learning didn't have to be wasted. Maybe my pain and what I was learning could accrue, not only to my benefit, but also to the benefit of others. Maybe I could share with others what I was learning about forgiveness, and maybe it could help others, because I'm pretty sure that virtually every person living in this broken world has struggled deeply with the question and challenge of forgiveness. So, in the midst of my own pain and struggle, I was slowly discovering a higher and transcendent meaning that was becoming greater than the pain itself. And that's why I was then compelled to write this book—because writing became a way for me to not only process and endure my own pain, to make some sense of it, and to find a deeper meaning in what had happened in my life, but also a way for me to enfold my pain and loss, and what I was learning, into my vocational calling to help others on the healing journey of their own hearts and lives.

If you'd like to listen to a short clip of Jordan Peterson on YouTube entitled, *Life is Suffering so get your act together*, that quite succinctly captures the essence of my motivation for writing *The Journey of Forgiveness*, you're invited to do so at this link:

https://www.youtube.com/watch?v=wLvd_ZbX1w0

About the Author

Tony Ingrassia is an author, counselor, and speaker. He received his bachelor's degree in biblical education from Florida Bible College, and his master's degree in counseling, MAC, from Covenant Theological Seminary. He's the founder and director of both Freedom Counseling Service, where he's available as a Licensed Professional Counselor, and The Power of Purity, which is a ministry devoted to helping men overcome issues of sexual compulsion and addiction to experience their sexual gift in a healthier way. Tony is the author of numerous books including *Stories*, *The Power of Purity*, and *God's Healing Path*.

Tony lives in St. Louis Missouri, and has three sons and four beautiful grandchildren. He owns a farm in north central Missouri which allows him to pursue his passion for hunting, fishing, and enjoying the great outdoors.

You can contact Tony at:
Tony Ingrassia
1529 Boones Lick Rd.
St. Charles, MO 63301
www.powerofpurity.org

Other Titles by Tony Ingrassia

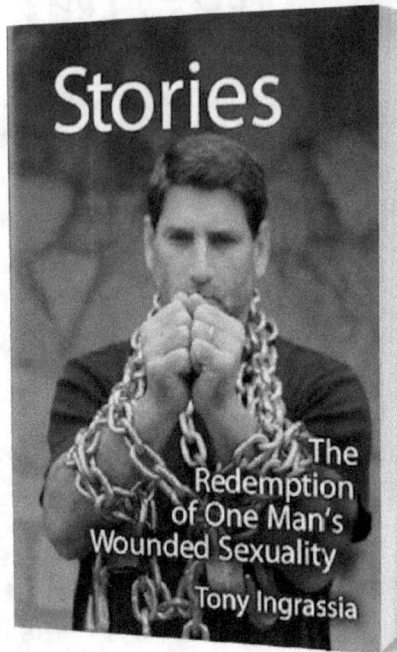

There's no greater issue central to manhood, or to masculinity, than the subject of sexuality. The relevance of this issue and the struggle it represents in the lives of many Christian men are almost universal, yet it remains one of the most neglected and avoided topics of discussion, especially in the Church. With our entire society relentlessly proclaiming the "gospel of sex," is it any wonder many Christian men struggle to control and express their sexuality in a way that's honoring to God?

In Stories, Tony Ingrassia shares his personal story of sexual struggle, sin, failure, pain, repentance, and redemption. Through the primary vehicle of his wounded sexuality, evil literally tried to destroy everything of significance in Tony's life, including his marriage, family, testimony, ministry, finances, and his very life. This is a brutally honest story that will inspire the hope that God really can "bind up the brokenhearted, proclaim freedom for the captives, and bring release from darkness for those who are in prison" (Isaiah 61:1). Stories is a unique book designed to help men in their struggle with this challenging area of life, to help women better understand the men in their lives, and to speak into the deepest places of the reader's heart as he finds greater freedom and redemption in his life, his marriage, and his sexuality.

THE POWER of PURITY

Freedom from the Roots of Sexual Sin

Tony Ingrassia

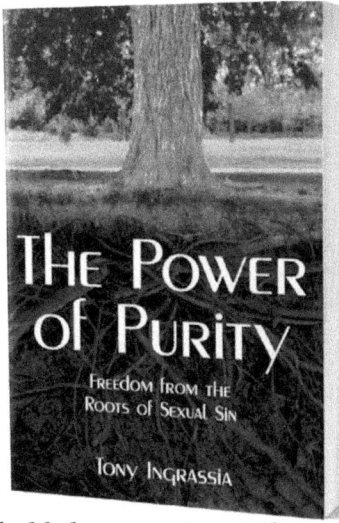

There's no issue more central to masculinity than sexuality, and it represents one of the most common and deepest struggles for many Christian men. Although Christian men know they're called to sexual purity, many find it difficult to achieve, as they struggle with various manifestations of sexual sin, including impure thoughts, compulsive masturbation, and internet pornography, among other such things. Many men are simply incapable of overcoming the compulsive tendencies they've struggled with for so long and are powerless to break free from the invisible chains that hold them captive. Why are so many good men struggling so deeply with their sexuality? Why do so many men find it so difficult to put their sexual struggles behind them and move into higher levels of sexual purity? The Power of Purity answers these questions along with many others.

The central message of this book is this: fruit comes from roots. Fruit is always the result of roots, and if a man is struggling with an ongoing manifestation of sexual compulsion, it's typically because of unholy sexual roots that he has never properly addressed. A man attempting to live in sexual purity, who has never dealt with such unholy roots, could be likened to an apple tree trying to no longer produce apples: impossible. As long as the unholy roots remain, unholy fruit will follow. The Power of Purity clearly exposes six unholy roots common to Christian men, and invites the reader into a process of repentance that will renounce the power and break the authority of each root in his life. Sexual purity does not have to remain a hopeless and unachievable dream. God has given the Christian man all things that pertain to life and godliness, and with God's help sexual purity is truly possible.

www.ingramcontent.com/pod-product-compliance
Lightning Source LLC
LaVergne TN
LVHW051303080426
835509LV00020B/3132